THE ROUGH GUIDE TO
Piano

**Whether you're a beginner or a pro,
whether you are about to buy a piano
or you want to learn more about the one
you already have – this book is for you.**

Hugo Pinksterboer

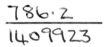

Publishing Details

This first edition published September 2000 by Rough Guides Ltd,
62–70 Shorts Gardens, London WC2H 9AB

Distributed by the Penguin Group:
Penguin Books Ltd, 27 Wrights Lane, London W8 5TZ
Penguin Putnam, Inc., 375 Hudson Street, New York, NY 10014
Penguin Books Australia Ltd, 487 Maroondah Highway, PO Box
257, Ringwood, Victoria 3134, Australia
Penguin Books Canada Ltd, 10 Alcorn Avenue, Toronto, Ontario,
Canada M4V 1E4
Penguin Books (NZ) Ltd, 182–190 Wairau Road, Auckland 10,
New Zealand

Typeset in Glasgow and Minion to an original design by
The Tipbook Company bv

Printed in The Netherlands by Hentenaar Boek bv, Nieuwegein

152pp

A catalogue record for this book is available from the British
Library.
1-85828-652-2

THE ROUGH GUIDE TO
Piano

Written by

Hugo Pinksterboer

ROUGH
GUIDES

THE ESSENTIAL TIPBOOK

Rough Guide Tipbook Credits

Journalist, writer and musician **Hugo Pinksterboer** has written hundreds of articles and reviews for international music magazines. He is the author of the reference work for cymbals (*The Cymbal Book*, Hal Leonard, US) and has written and developed a wide variety of musical manuals and courses.

Illustrator, designer and musician **Gijs Bierenbroodspot** has worked as an art director in magazines and advertising. While searching in vain for information about saxophone mouthpieces he came up with the idea for this series of books on music and musical instruments. Since then, he has created the layout and the illustrations for all of the books.

Acknowledgements

Concept, design and illustrations: Gijs Bierenbroodspot

Translation: MdJ Copy & Translation

Editor: Kim Burton

IN BRIEF

Have you been playing the piano for a while, or are you thinking of starting? Do you want to know more about the instrument you already have, or are you thinking about buying one? If so, this book will tell you everything you need to know about buying or renting a piano, and about what you need to look out for when choosing a new or secondhand instrument. It also covers such subjects as regular tuning and why it matters, maintenance, the history of the piano and some of its relatives, as well as many other matters.

Getting the most from your piano

That knowledge will help you make a good choice when you go to buy a piano. If you already have one, then read this book to get the most out of it. This book also explains all the jargon you're likely to come across, making it much easier for you to read more about the piano in books, magazines and brochures, or on the Internet.

Begin at the beginning

If you have only just started to play, or haven't yet begun, pay special attention to the first four chapters. Those who have been playing longer can skip ahead to chapter 5 if they prefer.

Glossary

Most of the piano terms you'll come across in this book are briefly explained in the glossary at the end. It also doubles as an index.

CONTENTS

1. THE PIANO

Performing a solo concert in a concert hall, accompanying a choir, a ballet company or a musical, or playing jazz, children's songs or pop songs. You can play music from today or from three hundred years ago, and you can do it at home, in a bar or in a studio. There are so many options open to you as a pianist.

As a pianist you can play an endless variety of musical styles, from centuries-old classical music to the very latest styles. Because the piano has been around for so long, and because it's effectively a complete orchestra in itself there's more music for the piano than practically any other instrument.

Lower and higher

A piano has lower notes than a double bass and higher notes than a piccolo, the very smallest flute. You can play the piano in a very slow and flowing style, like a violin, say, but you can also play it as though it were a drum kit. You can play note by note or play ten keys at once.

Accompaniments

One way in which a piano is like an orchestra is because you can play an accompaniment with one hand while playing a melody with the other. You can sing along too, and many pianists do, from Elton John to Tori Amos. Or you can accompany a singer or violinist, for instance: countless compositions have been written for piano together with another instrument.

Written at the piano

Because a piano is so versatile a lot of music has been written 'at the piano' by classical composers, pop musicians, jazz pianists, cabaret artists and all kinds of other musicians.

Playing by ear

On a piano, all the notes are easy to find. They're lined up side by side, from low to high. And there's a separate key for each note. That's why the piano is one of the easiest instruments to use if you want to play a tune by ear. If a note sounds too high, you move to the left and play a lower one. And the further you go to the right, the higher the note. Only singing is easier.

Four hundred pounds or more

A piano is one of the largest instruments you're likely to find in someone's home. It's nearly five feet wide and three feet high, and may be even bigger, and it's easily four hundred pounds (200kg) in weight. There's one big advantage to that: you'll never have to take your instrument with you when you perform. Which in turn has one big disadvantage: you can never be quite sure whether you'll be faced with a wonderful grand piano or an out-of-tune, tinny old upright with dodgy keys.

An upright piano

A grand piano

Grands

At most big concerts, whether classical, jazz or another style, the pianist plays a grand piano. Because it is a 'horizontal piano', a grand takes up much more space than an upright or vertical piano, even if it's a small model. Grands are more expensive than upright pianos too.

2. A QUICK TOUR

From the outside, a piano looks like little more than a big cabinet with a lot of keys, two or three pedals and a lid, but if you take a look inside you'll find many more parts. Just under ten thousand, in fact. This chapter introduces the most important parts, tells you what they are called and what they do, and explains the differences between upright pianos and grands.

Most pianos have eighty-eight keys divided into alternating groups of *two* or *three* black keys. This grouping makes all the notes very easy to find.

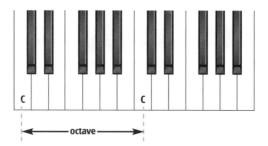

alternating groups of two and three black keys

The note C

Here are a couple of examples: the white key just to the left of two black keys is always a C. And the white key to the left of a group of three black keys is always an F.

Seven octaves

There are always eight white keys from one C to the next.

Such a group is called an octave. A piano keyboard always covers at least seven octaves.

Hammers and strings

Each key operates a hammer inside the piano. When you press the keys down, those hammers strike the strings. The harder you play, the harder they strike, and the louder it sounds. When you release the keys, the sound stops.

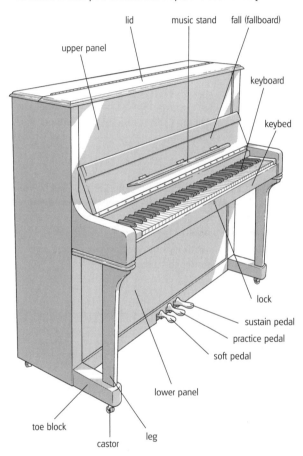

Pedals

Most pianos have two pedals, although some have three. If you press down the right-hand pedal, the strings that have already been struck continue sounding when the keys are released. When you use the left-hand pedal, everything sounds a little quieter.

Practice pedal

Some uprights have a third, middle pedal. Pressing this down moves a strip of felt between the strings and the hammers. This *practice* or *moderator pedal* allows you to practice without being heard in every room – or the house next door.

THE CABINET

Most upright pianos are between 40 and 52 inches (100–130cm) high. The width and the depth are pretty much the same for all instruments.

Music stand

On most uprights the *music stand* is on the inside of the *fall* or *fallboard,* which is often lockable. On others it is mounted on the *upper panel.*

Keybed

On taller pianos, the *keybed* is often supported by two legs. The keybed is also known as the *key slip* or *key-bottom.*

Castors and toe blocks

Most instruments with legs have wheels or *castors,* two at the back and two under the *toe blocks.*

Lid

When the *lid* is open everything sounds a little louder, brighter and more direct.

THE BACK

At the back of an upright you will usually find a framework made up of several thick posts, and behind it a large wooden board with wooden bars and handgrips attached to it. These posts, or *backposts,* serve to strengthen the instrument.

Soundboard

The wooden board behind the backposts is the *soundboard.* When the strings vibrate, the soundboard vibrates too. Without the soundboard, you would barely be able to hear the strings. It amplifies the sound of the piano in the same way as the soundbox or body of a guitar or a violin does. The soundboard is reinforced by a set of diagonal bars: the *ribs*.

Handgrips

The handgrips make it a little easier to move a piano. Only a little easier though, because even a small upright can easily weigh four hundred pounds (200kg).

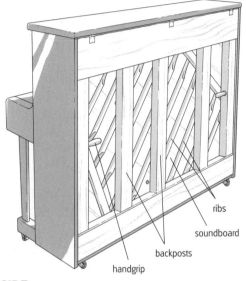

ribs

soundboard

backposts

handgrip

INSIDE

Most parts of a piano are inside. If you include every spring, pin and piece of felt, there are at least ten thousand.

Action

Most of the parts belong to the *action*, which makes the hammers strike the strings. The mechanism is ingenious, but easy to explain.

Jacks

The keys pivot in the middle, so as the front of a key is pressed down its back goes up. This flicks the *jack* upwards, sending the hammer moving towards the *string*.

Dampers

As the hammer travels towards the string the *damper* is removed from it. The moment you release the key the damper returns to the string and stops it sounding.

Ready for the next note

The jack springs back immediately after it has passed on its motion to the hammer. If it didn't, the hammer would remain pressed against the string, instead of just striking it briefly. As soon as you let go of the key, the jack returns to its place, ready for the next note.

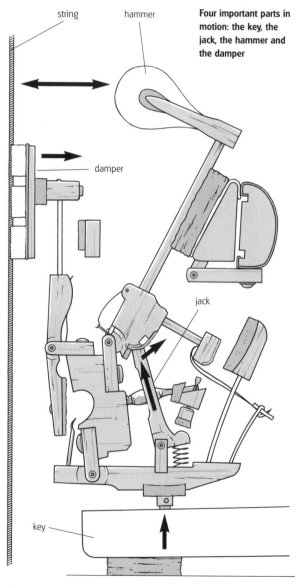

string

hammer

Four important parts in motion: the key, the jack, the hammer and the damper

damper

jack

key

Long and thick, or short and thin

A piano needs to have long, thick strings to produce the low notes. To make them extra thick, copper wire is wound around them. Stretching them across the cabinet diagonally saves a little space. The strings for the highest notes are short and thin.

One, two or three strings per note

Long, thick strings naturally sound fuller and louder and carry on sounding for longer than short, thin strings. To prevent them overbalancing the high ones the strings are arranged so that you actually strike three strings, all tuned to the same note, simultaneously when you play any key in the highest five octaves. In the lowest bass section, each hammer only strikes one string at a time, and in between there are a small number of notes which each have two identically-tuned strings. The sets of two or three identically-tuned strings are called *unisons*.

One hammer, one note. The three strings tuned to the same pitch

Twenty cars

A piano has around two hundred and twenty strings in total. Together, they exert a force of between thirty and forty thousand pounds (up to twenty tons), the weight of about twenty cars of average size.

Frame

To resist this huge tension pianos have a heavy, cast-iron frame. Together with the backposts, this frame or *plate* is the backbone of a piano.

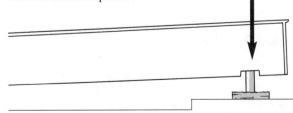

Tuning-pins

The strings are tuned by turning the *tuning-pins* or *wrest pins*, which are set into the *pinblock* (also called the *wrest plank*). You can't always see the pinblock, a sturdy block made up of layers of wood: it's usually hidden behind the frame.

Bass and treble

The strings are divided into three groups. From the top left the *bass strings* run diagonally downwards. The next group of strings is the *low treble* or *tenor*, and the highest octaves are called the *high treble*.

Bridges

All strings run over a *bridge*: a long, narrow piece of wood which transmits the vibrations of the strings to the sound-board. The bass strings have their own fairly short bridge.

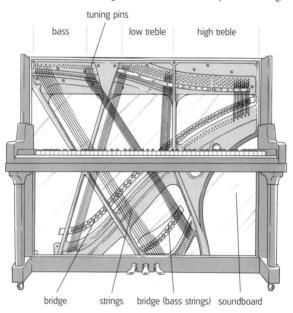

tuning pins

bass   low treble   high treble

bridge   strings   bridge (bass strings)   soundboard

GRAND PIANO

You can think of a grand piano as a horizontal upright piano. Or perhaps better, since the grand was invented first (see chapter 11), look on the upright piano as a vertical grand.

Bigger and heavier

Even the smallest grand piano takes up more space than the biggest upright. The very biggest grands, which are some nine feet long, weigh half a ton or more. The smallest models (baby grands) are half that length.

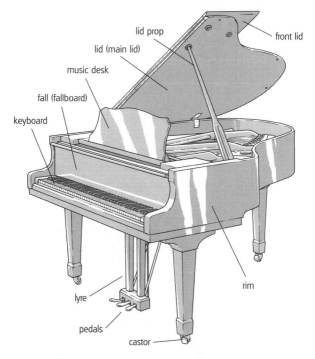

lid prop

front lid

lid (main lid)

music desk

fall (fallboard)

keyboard

rim

lyre

pedals

castor

Main lid and front lid

The *lid* of a grand piano consists of two parts: the *main lid* and the *front lid*. When you open the front lid, the music stand becomes visible.

With the lid open

The best way to hear what a grand piano has to offer is to play it with the lid open. At performances, a grand piano is usually positioned so that the sound is reflected towards the audience off the inside of the lid.

Strings and frame

When a grand piano is open, the strings and the frame can be clearly seen, as can the soundboard beneath them. Grand pianos have the same number of strings as upright pianos, and like them, their bass strings run cross-wise above the other strings: both instruments are *cross-strung* or *overstrung*.

Action

An important difference between uprights and grands is that the hammers of a grand piano strike upwards, rather than forwards. That makes everything a little simpler because gravity does its bit: when you release the keys the dampers and the hammers fall back into place by themselves.

More control

This type of action, together with the slightly longer keys, mean that you have more control over the sound of a grand piano than over that of an upright. It's easier to go from very soft to very loud, for example. Playing rapidly repeated notes is also easier on a grand piano.

Pedals

Most modern grand pianos have three pedals, which are attached to the *lyre*. The right-hand pedal has the same function on a grand as on an upright piano.

Left-hand pedal

The left-hand pedal works differently. If you press down this *una corda pedal*, all the keys shift slightly to the right, and the action and the hammers move with them. As a result, the hammers strike one less string in each unison. This not only makes the sound softer, but a little milder too.

Sostenuto pedal

The middle pedal is the *sostenuto* pedal. If you play one or more keys and press this pedal, only those notes will sustain. All the other keys work in the normal way: the strings are damped as soon as the keys are released.

THE OCTAVES

A piano keyboard has enough keys for seven octaves and a bit more. That means there are at least seven keys for each note – seven keys which give the note G, for instance (one per octave). And some notes even have eight keys. To avoid confusion, each octave and each key is given its own name.

Middle C

The most important key to remember is the C in the middle of the keyboard. This is called middle C or c1. It's the first note of the one-line octave.

The A

The A which most instruments tune to is a1, slightly to the right of c1. The names of the other notes are shown in the drawing below. The notes in the lowest three octaves are written in capitals, the others in small letters.

Other ways

There are other ways to indicate the various octaves. Two examples: middle C is sometimes called C4 (it's the fourth C on a piano keyboard) or C40 (it's the 40th key).

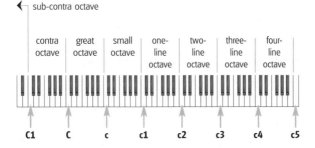

Other instruments

To give you an impression of how wide the range of a piano really is, the illustration shows you how it compares with the ranges of a few other well-known instruments.

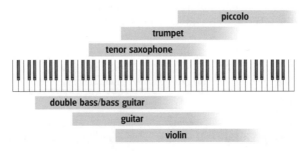

3. LEARNING TO PLAY

Is it difficult to learn to play the piano? In one respect, no, because all the keys are so conveniently placed side by side. In another respect yes, not least because you need to be able to develop the skill of playing two independent parts at the same time, one with your left hand and one with your right. This chapter describes the difficulties and the advantages, the question of learning to read music, and talks about lessons and practice.

If you've heard a tune somewhere, it's often easier to pick it out by ear on a piano than on another instrument, since all the notes are easy to find and you can find them with just one finger.

All ten fingers
Still, to play the piano properly you need more than one finger. You usually play the melody with your right hand and the accompaniment with your left, although it can be the other way around. Or you play two 'voices', one with

Sonatine, M. Clementi, Opus 36, No. 1 (fragment)

The upper staff shows the music for the right hand; the lower staff the music for the left hand.

14

the left hand and one with the right. You can also play big chords, with four or even five notes per hand.

A duet
In a way, even when you play alone, you perform a kind of 'duet' on the piano: you can picture your left hand as one musician, and your right hand as another. That's what allows you to do so much with the instrument. The drawback is that a pianist needs to be able to read the notes for both hands at the same time. That does take a little while to learn, but it's actually not that hard.

Always in tune
One of the great advantages of a piano is that, if the instrument is properly tuned, you'll never sound out of tune: you don't have to play the notes in exactly the right place or make them sound 'right', as you do on a violin, a sax or a trumpet. Even so, a good pianist will get a better sound from a piano than a bad one.

LESSONS
Of course there are pianists who have never had a teacher, but by far the majority started out by having lessons, whether they play classical music or something very different.

Music school or private?
Just about every music school has a piano teacher, and of course there are private teachers too. At a music school, you often have to pay a whole year's fees in one go. You may be able to pay a private teacher per month, or even per lesson.

Collectives and music schools
You may also want to check whether there are any teachers' collectives or music schools in your vicinity. These may be able to offer you the chance of ensemble playing, master-classes and clinics as well as normal lessons, and can be considerably cheaper.

Prices
The prices of lessons at music schools vary a lot: £70–500/ $100–700 a year or more. How much you pay can depend on your age, the number of lessons you have a month, the

length of a lesson, your or your parents' income. There may be discount schemes. Private teachers cost around £15–40/$25–75 an hour.

Ask first

If you go to a school or a teacher, don't just ask what it costs. Here are a few things it is useful to know.

- Ask if you can have a trial lesson first. Then you can see if it clicks between you and the teacher. And between you and the piano!
- Will your teacher expect you to study for several hours a day, or will they continue to teach you even if you only manage to practice for a few hours each week?
- Do you need to buy a shelf-full of books, or will the teacher supply teaching materials?
- Is the teacher familiar with the type of music you want to learn to play?

Locating a teacher

Piano shops may have a list of private teachers they can refer you to, or you could ask the Musicians' Union, which has a teachers' register. Some players have found great teachers simply by asking performers they heard at a concert. Check the classified ads in newspapers, in music magazines, shop-windows or on supermarket bulletin boards, or try the *Yellow Pages*.

READING MUSIC

If you have lessons then you'll learn to read music too. It's not really that hard. What is a little trickier is the fact that, when you are playing piano, you need to keep an eye on two staves at once.

Without reading music

Of course there are fine pianists who can't read a note, but can hear a piece of music and can repeat it at once, by ear. And there have even been countless pieces 'written' on the piano by musicians who couldn't read a note either.

Klavar-stave

You can also put music onto paper without using notes, simply by indicating which keys are to be played (see example on page 74). One of the better-known methods is to write the notes down in a *Klavar-stave*, using a system invented by Cornelius Pot, a Dutch engineer. Far less music has been published in this way than in the regular staff notation.

PRACTICE

You can play without learning to read music. You can learn without a teacher. But there's no substitute for practice. And when you practice the piano everyone can hear you unless you mute the sound one way or another: a piano is one of the loudest instruments there is.

Thirty minutes or eight hours a day?

How long you need to practice depends on how gifted you are and what you want to achieve. It's true that many top pianists have spent years practising between four and eight hours a day, but playing for thirty minutes to an hour each day will help you make good progress.

Plenty of volume

A piano produces more volume than most other instruments, and the sound travels through walls and floors to reach your neighbours and the other rooms in the house. How do you keep everyone happy?

Practice pedal

Many newer uprights have a *practice pedal* (see pages 64–65), which allows you to make the piano sound a great deal quieter. Practice pedals can sometimes be retro-fitted (built in afterwards) if your piano doesn't have one.

Agree when to play

If you occasionally want to play 'no holds barred', without dampers, then it may be worth talking to your neighbours and others in your house to agree set practice times. This often works well and costs nothing.

Stop the sound travelling

You can also take steps to stop more of the sound travelling through walls and floors. If you have a concrete floor, it can help if you place the instrument on special *castor cups* (see page 88) or other sound-absorbing material. There is little point in placing this type of material between the piano and the wall: the main thing you achieve is to make the instrument sound dull. There are specialist books on the subject if you want to know more.

Silent pianos

You'll play a lot more quietly if your piano has a *muting system*. This system makes sure the hammers don't quite touch the strings. You can still hear what you are playing by using a pair of headphones connected to a *sound module*: a small box mounted under the keyboard. The way this all works and the systems available are described in chapter 7, *Silent, Player and Digital Pianos*.

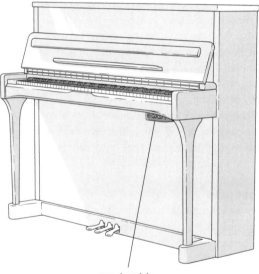

sound module

Digital piano

If you want to play silently, you can also buy a digital piano. Instead of strings it has digital recordings (*samples*) of the sound of one or more pianos, just like a sound module. The latest digital pianos sound more and more like ordinary pianos, but they still don't play or sound quite the same. Want to know more? See chapter 7, and if you are still curious, read *The Rough Guide to Keyboard and Digital Piano*.

Practising with CDs

Most pianists practice using books, but there are other options available. For instance, you can buy CDs on which the piano part has been left out, so you can play with a full orchestra, or with another pianist, or play a duet with a violinist without actually needing to find a real musician to join you.

Computerized lessons

Digital pianos and sound modules can usually be directly connected to a computer. Add a special program and you can use your computer as a private teacher. You can also use your computer for practice without this type of connection: for instance, there is software that can demonstrate pieces for you or teach you how to read music, or which you can program to simulate a complete band or an orchestra accompanying you.

Video lessons

Like most computer programs, most video piano lessons are intended for pianists who want to play in jazz, blues, rock or other styles. Such videos usually have a playing time of thirty minutes to an hour.

Metronomes

As a pianist you have to be able to keep time, just like every other musician. That's why it's good to practice with a

Two mechanical (clockwork) and two electronic metronomes

metronome now and again: a device which produces bleeps or ticks, letting you hear exactly whether you are playing too fast or too slowly.

Playing and listening

And finally: listen to as much music as you can. One of the best ways to learn to play is to watch other musicians at work. Whether they are living legends or local amateurs, you can learn something from every performance. But the best way of all to learn is to play as often as you can, alone or with others, and practice hard.

4. BUYING OR RENTING?

Even the cheapest new pianos cost £1000/$1500 or more. On the other hand, a good piano will last for decades and will keep its value well. If that's too much money to spend in one go, or if you want to try an instrument out for a while first, you can rent one. This chapter is about prices, exactly what you're paying for, buying, renting and leasing new or secondhand instruments, and about piano shops. Everything you need to look out for once you go into the shop is described in chapter 5, *A Good Piano*.

When you consider all that wood and all those thousands of parts, then a thousand or two isn't all that much money to ask for a new piano. Yet the cheapest instruments are available at that price. You'll pay around ten times as much for the most expensive.

Grand pianos
The prices of grand pianos are a lot higher. These start somewhere around £7000/$10,000, and you'll easily pay a hundred thousand for the most expensive model.

Long-lasting
Because they last a long time good pianos have a high trade-in value, sometimes as much as you paid for it in the first place if you're exchanging the instrument for a more expensive one.

A decent piano
If you are looking for a new upright piano which isn't too

expensive, sounds good, stays in tune, is well regulated and will work without problems for at least the first ten years, expect to pay £2200–3000/$3000–4000 or more. If you want to pay less, you can't set your sights as high.

A richer tone

The difference between expensive and cheap pianos is not easy to see. What are you actually paying for if you spend more money? In the first place a better tone, of course. More expensive instruments usually sound 'richer', in a word.

Taller and 'bigger'

The most expensive uprights are usually around four feet tall, and the cheapest a little over three. The taller an upright is, the 'bigger' it usually sounds – but there are also very good short uprights for sale, and not so good tall ones.

Better materials

More expensive pianos have had more work done by hand, and more expensive materials are used. That means better wood, which has been seasoned for years so that it won't shrink or expand. It also means better felt for the hammers and the dampers, more expensive strings, and more carefully applied lacquer, which will last longer. All these things make an instrument sound better and more enjoyable to play, and help it last and hold its value for longer.

More work

A piano that costs more will – usually – have had more work done on it. For instance, a good piano will have been tuned up to ten times and carefully regulated before it leaves the factory.

Bad pianos

Is there such as thing as a bad piano? Yes. It might be a piano which goes out of tune quickly, or a piano made from wood which has not been properly seasoned, so that keys, panels and other parts may warp. Unfortunately, these are all things you are unlikely to be able to see when the instrument is brand new and standing in the shop. A few tips: read up a lot and ask plenty of advice beforehand, go to several shops, and ask about what is and what isn't covered by the guarantee.

Upright or grand?

Many pianists would prefer a grand piano if money and space permit. After all, the upright was invented mainly because grands take up so much room. So is a grand piano always better? Not necessarily, and certainly not if you're talking about instruments at roughly the same price. Some people would still prefer a small, affordable grand piano, others will choose an upright because a particular instrument simply sounds better or is more playable, or both. And there will always be pianists who walk into a shop to buy a grand and walk out having bought an upright, or the other way around.

A little more

Of course, the price of a grand piano depends on the quality, but also on the dimensions. If you go from a five-foot grand to one a foot longer in the same series, it'll easily cost £1500/$2500 more – and when it comes to the very best instruments, the price difference is likely to be two or even three times as great.

SECONDHAND

Instead of a new instrument, you can buy a secondhand upright or grand piano, either through a classified ad in the newspaper, from a piano shop or from a piano tuner.

Appraisal

If somebody is selling you their own piano secondhand, it's safest to get it appraised (valued) first. Even if it's a cheap instrument – if a £300/$500 piano really needs a lot of work, it can easily cost twice as much to make it truly playable. An appraisal usually costs between £35 and £100/$75 and $150. The appraisal report you get will also tell you what needs to be done to the instrument, and what it'll cost.

In the shop

You can find good used pianos in piano shops, but also through piano tuners or technicians. Usually they will already have been inspected and regulated. Prices often start at around £1000/$1500.

The right price

Buying secondhand from a shop, a piano tuner or a technician has other advantages. For example, you can usually choose from a number of instruments, and come back if you have questions or if problems crop up and you should be able to depend on not paying more than the instrument is worth.

Guarantee

What's more, you'll usually get a guarantee. Some guarantee certificates even show if any parts have been replaced or reconditioned.

Old and nearly new

Just like with cars, some of the instruments on sale are old and others are nearly new. You can sometimes buy really old pianos for next to nothing. Are they good enough to start on? Maybe, but if a piano doesn't play well and is hard to tune properly, then starting is as far as most people will get. You'll find technical tips on buying secondhand instruments on page 67.

RENTING AND LEASING

Many piano shops rent out instruments too, from around £35/$25 a month. The cost of rental increases with the selling price of the instrument.

Tuning

The amount of the rental also partly depends on what is included in the fee. For instance, who pays for tuning – you'll probably need to have your piano tuned two or three times a year – and who pays the transport costs and the insurance?

Deducting the fee

If you eventually decide to buy the instrument some or all the rental you have paid up till then may be deducted from the price. The size of the discount can vary from shop to shop, and the length of the rental period may also play a role. For instance, one shop will charge you interest on the amount you have not yet paid in rental, another won't. So, always read a rental or rent-to-own agreement through carefully before you sign it.

Leasing

Some makers, importers and distributors offer special finance lease deals with a relatively low rate of interest. Leasing may be a good solution if you are sure you want to buy a particular instrument but can't afford it straight away.

THE SHOP

The more instruments a shop has on display, the harder it can be to choose one. On the other hand, the wider the choice of instruments, the better the chance that you'll find exactly what you're looking for. What is especially important is that you are given the time and space to play yourself, to look and to listen, and that you talk to salespeople who know a lot about the instrument, who play themselves and who enjoy their work.

Sound advice

Good information is crucial when it comes to pianos. Because it's not easy to see the difference between various models and because they are expensive instruments, which you want to last you for years. Good information is also important because an instrument may only show its true quality after months, or even years.

Discussing it

This book offers a good deal of the information you need, but without proper advice in the shop choosing an instrument remains difficult. A good salesperson can help you to make a good choice by discussing things like the type of music you play, how long you've been playing for, the piano you're used to, and the room where the instrument will be kept – and they won't simply tell you which piano you should choose.

Tuned and ready to play

In a good shop, all the instruments will be in tune and ready to play. You shouldn't buy a piano that hasn't been tuned, because you won't be able to hear what it really sounds like. What about a piano that doesn't play well? The problem may simply be poor regulation, so if it seems attractive in other ways you should definitely wait until the instrument has been regulated before you choose – and be sure to try it again first.

Go back

Most piano shops won't mind if you go back a few times, and you'll probably need to before you can make a final choice. Many buyers will visit a number of different shops over a period of a week or so, not only to compare instruments of different makes, but also the stories that go with them. Have you fallen in love with a piano at first sight? That's often a good sign. Still, it's not a bad idea to come back the next day to listen to it again.

Exchanging or trying out

Pianos hardly ever sound the same in the shop as in the living room. It's possible, though unlikely, that when the piano is finally delivered to your home you will be disappointed by its tone. Some shops will allow you to exchange the instrument, and some shops will even let you try the instrument out at home. Naturally, you'll have to meet the cost of transport yourself (see page 99).

That one

No two pianos sound exactly the same. For this reason, some shop owners go so far as to choose the exact instruments they want from an importer, a distributor or factory. And because every piano does sound a little bit different, make sure you have the same piano that you played on in the shop delivered to you, and not an 'identical' one from their warehouse. Every instrument has a serial number, which you can have noted on your receipt to be on the safe side.

Part-exchange

Many shops offer a part-exchange guarantee. The trade-in allowance may be worth as much as the full price of the first piano, but do ask beforehand how much more expensive the new instrument needs to be. Some shops offer part-exchange deals for secondhand instruments too.

Guarantee

Most new pianos are guaranteed for five years or more, although exactly what falls under the guarantee may differ. If the guarantee only covers the material costs of certain parts, it's not much good to you: the labour involved in replacing a part often costs more than the part itself.

Maintenance agreement

Sometimes a guarantee is only valid if you sign a maintenance agreement. If you then fail to comply with that agreement, your guarantee may lapse. Your guarantee may also be affected if you install a humidifier system (see page 97), or decide not to. Again: reading the agreement is important, and it's a good idea to ask other shops what their conditions are.

FINALLY

A piano is one of the few instruments that you don't tune yourself. Usually the tuner needs to come by twice or three times a year: expect to pay £30–50/$50–75 a time. You can read more about other costs in chapters 8 and 9.

Take someone along

When you go looking for a new instrument take along someone else who can play the piano. That way both of you can listen and discuss things with each other, and there are many other advantages: see chapter 6, *Playing and Listening*.

Leaflets and magazines

If you want to know all the ins and outs, then start by taking all the brochures from every shop – including those of the most expensive makes. There are also a number of magazines for pianists, and many books where you can find out more, as well as various useful Web sites. Details of some are given at the end of this book.

Music fairs

One last tip: if there is a music fair or convention being held anywhere near you, go. You may well find many different makes of uprights and grand pianos displayed side by side, which makes it easy to compare them. You'll also meet scores of pianists, so you'll always learn something.

5. A GOOD PIANO

How do pianos differ, one from another? What difference does the height of the instrument make, for example, and what can you tell by looking at the cabinet, the keyboard or the hammers And what about all those other things you hear or read about? This chapter is about all the differences you can see or feel, and on how they affect a piano's tone.

Almost every single component, from the backposts to the strings and the soundboard to the dampers, makes some contribution to the tone of the instrument. Where a piano is different from most other instruments is that you can't simply replace any of its parts and expect to influence or adjust the tone in the way a saxophonist can experiment with different mouthpieces and reeds, or a violinist with strings and rosins.

Adjustments
However, it is possible to adjust the tone of a piano to some extent by making the hammers softer or harder, and you can even have the strings, the hammers and other parts replaced. Mind you, these are all jobs for a professional. You can read more further on in this chapter and in chapter 10.

The sum of the parts
In a piano, the tone is the sum of all the parts. No one instrument is ever better than another just because a better type of wood has been used – what matters more is whether that type of wood suits that particular instrument.

Big or small uprights

The very smallest uprights are about three feet high, and the tallest about a foot higher, although you may occasionally come across uprights which are even taller. The height is important for the tone: a taller instrument has a bigger soundboard and longer strings, producing a 'bigger' sound and more volume. It's the same with grand pianos. That's one of the reasons why most concert halls have a grand piano around nine foot long.

Louder, but just as soft

It's easy to hear the difference between a small and a tall piano of the same quality. The tall one has a more power-ful, broader, richer and fuller tone and, if you play with more force, more volume – yet it can sound just as soft as the smaller model. A tall piano often feels different from a small one to the player, since in a small instrument the action has to be adapted to fit the reduced dimensions.

Size isn't everything

Of course, the quality of an instrument is as important as its height. An expensive piano which is four feet (120cm) high can easily sound 'bigger' and richer than a taller but much cheaper instrument. What if you have to choose between two models of the same price, one a little taller and the other a little shorter? Then buy the piano which sounds the best and which you feel most comfortable playing. In other words, the size alone doesn't tell you everything.

How much more

How much you pay for extra height and tone depends, among other things, on the make and the price range. To give you an idea: if you pay around £2200/$3000 for an instrument that is 43 inches (110cm) high, one make which is four inches taller may cost £700/$1000 extra while another make would cost more than £1600/$2500 extra. Why? Perhaps because the second manufacturer uses a better action for the taller model, and the first one does not.

The widest choice

The widest choice of instruments, regardless of price range or quality, is available in instruments between 45 inches

(115cm) and 50 inches (125cm) high, the most popular size for an upright. In most cases the difference that a couple of inches make will be barely noticeable. You may also find that some taller instruments simply have an extra high cabinet. Of course, they don't sound any bigger than a piano with a smaller cabinet but the same size soundboard.

Spinets and full-size uprights

The smallest pianos, with a height below about 40 inches (100cm), are called spinet pianos. Console pianos are taller, and the largest upright pianos are called studio or full-size uprights – some even make a distinction between the latter two. There are no set sizes for these types. For instance, some say that studio pianos range from 43 to 47 inches, others use the name to describe pianos of 49 inches and above.

Space

A tall piano looks much bigger than a small one. Even so, tall ones usually take up the same amount of floor space. Most pianos are between 22 and 24 inches (55–60cm) deep, and the differences in width are also very minor.

A big upright or a small grand?

Does a grand piano always sound 'bigger' than an upright? No, although it often seems that way, because grands are usually played with the lid open and uprights with it closed. What about the size of the soundboard? The soundboard of a five and a half feet (175cm) long grand piano is about the same size as a four feet two inch (130cm) upright, so you would only expect to hear a difference if the grand is longer than that.

Choosing

Having said that, there are some important differences. One is that the sound of a grand piano with its lid open spreads out freely in all directions from the soundboard, which is much less the case with an upright. Many pianists feel they are more 'inside the sound' when they play a grand piano. And yet pianists sometimes opt for an upright when they were originally looking for a grand. So, if you have enough money and space for either, it comes down to playing, listening and comparing.

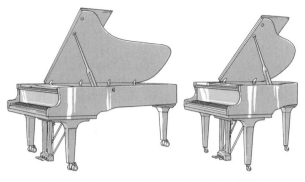

A nine-foot (275 cm) concert grand piano and a five-foot (150 cm) baby grand

Grand piano names

The smallest grand pianos, between roughly five foot (150cm) and five foot six (165cm) in length, are often called *baby* or *boudoir grands*. *Medium grands* are slightly longer, while models of around seven foot (225cm) are often called *small concert grands*. The largest models are the 'proper' *concert grands*, measuring about eight foot (275cm), although a few makers produce even larger instruments.

The difference

To give you an idea: in a concert grand, the soundboard is nearly twice as big as in a baby grand, and the longest string is about twice as long – and you can certainly hear that difference. You can read more about soundboards and strings later in this chapter.

THE OUTSIDE

Uprights and grand pianos come in a wide variety of styles and finishes; from high-gloss black to wood finishes in many different colours, and from simple designs with controlled lines to impressively carved Rococo models.

High-gloss and silk-gloss

Most high-gloss black or *ebonized* instruments are treated with a thick coat of polyester lacquer. This type of lacquer is pretty tough, and small scratches or other minor damage are quite easy to polish away. The advantage of silk-gloss (*satin-finish*) instruments is that they don't show up dust, fingerprints and dirt as clearly.

Transparent or coloured

Transparent varnishes allow you to see the veneer, the thin layer of wood used on the outside of an instrument. Woods commonly used for the veneer include oak, mahogany, cherry and walnut, or combinations of several different types. Each type of wood has its own hue and pattern. When it comes to solid colours, high-gloss polyester lacquer is normally used. Black is the most popular of the solid colours, followed by white.

Open pore

On open pore instruments you can both see and feel the wood, as the grain has not been lacquered smooth or filled.

Wax

There are also matt-finish instruments available in which the wood is protected with wax instead of lacquer.

Synthetic

Some cheap pianos are finished with a synthetic outer layer instead of a thin layer of wood. This so-called *photoprint* is cheaper and easier to maintain.

French polish

French-polished instruments are finished with shellac, a natural lacquer with a warm, silky sheen. This type of lacquer is most common on older instruments, although there are makes which still offer new French-polished pianos. Shellac is more easily damaged and more expensive than polyester lacquer (see also page 90).

Custom designs

Some makers build pianos in custom colours and designs. The drawback is that you can't play a piano like this before you decide to buy it. Some shops also have instruments lacquered themselves: you first choose a piano and then they arrange for it to be lacquered.

Good and smooth

It is hard to see how well or how thickly the lacquer has been applied, but you can check to see how smoothly the instrument has been polished. Look especially carefully at the reflections in the lacquer.

Inside

The panels are almost always lacquered on the inside too. This protects the wood and reduces the chances of warping.

More expensive or not

With one make, an ebonized finish is more expensive than a satin finish, with the next make it's the other way around. Sometimes it depends on the type of wood used to finish the instrument: cherry costs more than oak, for example. You always pay extra for special colors and lacquers.

Details

There are manufacturers who make their instruments more attractive with details such as walnut strips around the edges, upper panels divided into fields or decorated with figures, chrome-finish instead of gold-coloured (brass) pedals, hinges and locks or – especially on grands – special woods on the inside of the cabinet. Bird's-eye maple, a densely patterned type of wood, is a well-known example.

Matching your interior

Many manufacturers also produce instruments to match interiors in a particular style. These may be Chippendale

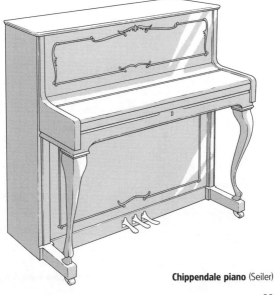

Chippendale piano (Seiler)

Rococo grand (Blüthner)

uprights, for instance, with artfully twisted legs and other ornate features, or heavily decorated grands in the Rococo style. At the other end of the scale, there are instruments designed for uncluttered modern interiors. Some manufacturers offer a choice of three, four or more styles for each series of pianos.

Modern piano (Sauter)

Decorations

Apart from the colour and the height, pianos may have many other minor differences which you'll only notice if you know where to look. A few examples: the corners of the keybed are sometimes a little more rounded, or a little more angular. The edges of the lids may be sawn straight, or they may be curved. The legs may run straight down, or be a little wider at the top, and they may be round, square or double.

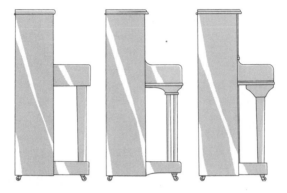

The little differences, if you know where to look for them

With or without legs

Uprights have three basic styles of cabinet. On smaller upright pianos the upper panel is often slanted backwards and there are no legs under the keybed. More highly

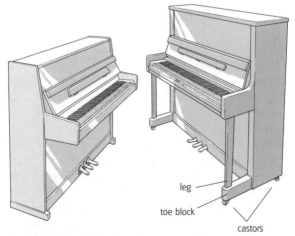

leg

toe block

castors

On upright pianos without legs, the upper panel is often slanted slightly backwards

ornamented 'Decorator style' instruments often have legs that extend all the way to the floor instead of being set into toe blocks like the so-called institutional- or professional-style pianos. Such legs are easily damaged, so be extra careful when you move the piano. Of course, you will also find combinations of these styles.

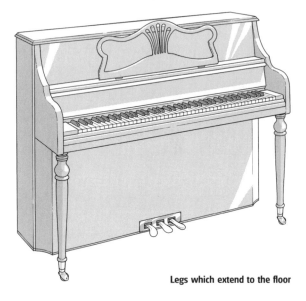

Legs which extend to the floor

Castors

Castors make an upright a little easier to shift around a room, but you shouldn't really use them to move it any distance. A tip: castors make the instrument look about half an inch taller than it really is. If there are no castors on an upright, you can have them fitted for around £100–150/$100–150, or a little more if the piano is already in your home. Another tip: the pedals can easily end up slightly too high if you have castors fitted.

Wheels

If a piano needs to be moved regularly, you need bigger wheels, or even better a sturdy *piano trolley*. Larger wheels are usually fitted to so-called *school pianos*, which have other extras like protective brackets, a lock for the fall and sometimes even a wooden plate to protect the sound-board. There are also wheels of various sizes for grand pianos, sometimes fitted with a brake.

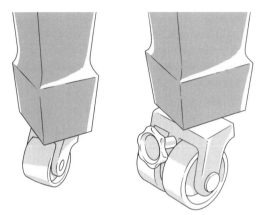

Grand piano wheels with and without brake

Higher keyboard, higher seat

If a piano has had wheels fitted, the keyboard will be raised, which usually means you need your seat to be a little higher (see page 86). Even without wheels, the height varies quite a lot: the height of the white keys varies between 26 and 28 inches (66–72cm), and that's more than it looks on paper. If the keyboard is low, the piano can be supported by castor cups (see page 88) – but make sure the pedals don't end up too high.

Mind your knees

The bottom of the keybed can also be much higher on one instrument than the next. The difference can be as much as four inches, or even more. A low model can be awkward if you have long legs.

LIDS, CABINETS AND BACKPOSTS

The large panels and posts of a piano are not the most important components when you are choosing an instrument, but there are a few things worth knowing before you buy.

Fall

On most upright pianos, the fall consists of two hinged parts. That's easier to make than a curved, one-piece fall. Some grand pianos have a *soft-fall* or *soft-close fall* with a system that stops it from slamming shut.

Caps

Some falls rest against two rubber caps when open to prevent the lacquer being damaged. Just to be on the safe side, always check that the fall opens easily and closes without rubbing.

Locked

If the fall doesn't have a built-in lock, you can buy a special U-shaped lock which fits around it. There are also built-in locks that lock it from the side.

Music stands

Most pianos have a music stand which is about 24" to 34" (60–80cm) wide. The wider models can hold four sheets side by side. To stop the sheet music from sliding off, music stands may have ridges or a raised edge, or be lined with felt, leather or imitation leather. There are also pianos with a music stand above the fall, so that the music stays where it is when you close the instrument. These stands may extend almost the whole width of the instrument.

Main Lid

You can open the main lid if you want to make the sound of an upright piano a little more direct. On some pianos

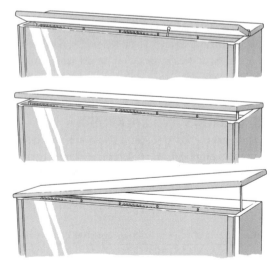

Different lids: a hinge in the middle, at the back and at the side

only the front half of the lid opens, others have lids hinged at the back, and still others *grand-style lids*, hinged at the side.

More volume

To get a little more volume, for instance if they want to play with a drummer, pianists sometimes take off the entire upper panel. That's easily done and doesn't require any tools. Please note that there is a risk that the backs of the hammers will now hit the fall. You can easily solve that problem by removing that as well. However, that does mean you remove your music stand as well, and that you risk damaging the action.

Openings

Some pianos have special openings to make the tone a bit fuller or more direct. These might be at the back, just under the lid, for instance. The occasional instrument has part of its upper panel made of cloth, or sports a kind of grille set into the lower panel.

Grand pianos: the front-lid

Many grand pianos have rubber caps glued onto the front-lid to prevent it from touching the main-lid when you open it. Such caps are always visible when the front-lid is closed, and it's barely possible to remove them without damaging the lacquer. Instead of these caps, some instruments have special little cushions that do the same job.

Music stands on grands

The music stand on a grand sits under the front-lid and can often be set in three or four different positions. So-called *openwork* stands, with a type of ornate carving, are only really a feature on certain older instruments. The music stand is attached to the *music shelf* by hinges.

Completely open

If necessary, you can slide the music shelf out of the instrument completely, for instance so that it can be tuned. Some pianists who don't use sheet music remove the music shelf permanently: this allows the instrument to sound a fraction more 'open', but it's a difference that affects the player more than the listener.

CHAPTER 5

Completely closed

You can go the other way too: if you want a grand piano to produce as little volume as possible, remove the music shelf, close the front-lid and place the shelf on top.

Lid

The lid (also called the *top*) can usually be opened in two positions. Very occasionally the *lid prop*, which holds it up, even allows for three: in the lowest one, the lid is barely open. Some grands have a big round knob on the side to operate a hook, which holds the lid in place when the instrument is being transported.

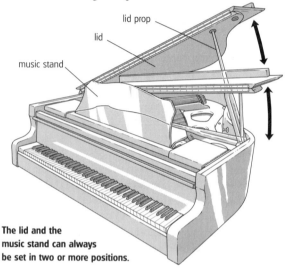

The lid and the music stand can always be set in two or more positions.

Backposts

At the back of the piano there are often between three and six thick backposts which give the instrument extra solidity. The number of posts required and their thickness mainly depends on how the rest of the instrument is constructed. Some smaller uprights don't have backposts at all, but have a heavier frame. Building an instrument without backposts is cheaper, and makes the cabinet some two to four inches (5–10cm) less deep.

Tone collector

The 'backposts' on grand pianos are referred to as *braces*, and they come in all kinds of variations, for example the

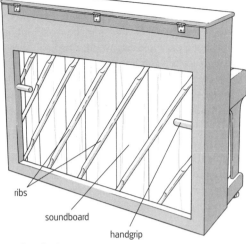

ribs

soundboard

handgrip

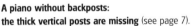

A piano without backposts:
the thick vertical posts are missing (see page 7).

tone collector, in which the posts all converge at a single point. Of course, while it can certainly affect the tone, you shouldn't choose or reject a particular instrument just because of the arrangement of the backposts, the number of posts or the exact dimensions of other parts, large or small.

Spruce or beech
The type of wood used for the backposts is another much discussed subject. For instance, some experts say posts made of solid spruce make the tone a little warmer, whereas mahogany allegedly helps produce a slightly stronger tone. Ultimately, the type of wood chosen was the one the manufacturer decided was the best suited, for reasons of tone, price or strength – and probably all three.

Upright cabinet
The panels, top and lid of an upright piano are often made from laminated planks composed of layers of poplar or birch. Chipboard (flakeboard) or MDF (Multi-Density Fibreboard), a very heavy material made of very fine wood fibres, is sometimes used on cheaper models. It's usually impossible to tell exactly which material has been used, not least because the outer layers and edges are often made of solid wood even if the rest isn't.

Moisture

Some of these cheaper panels are more resistant to warping than solid wood panels. This may be worth taking into account if you are intending to put the piano somewhere where temperature and humidity vary a lot (see also page 62). The drawback with chipboard is that it is less sturdy, and so the screws that support the music stand and other parts can come loose more easily.

Rim

The cabinet (of an upright) or the *rim* (of a grand) can influence the tone of some makes. Maple or beech are often used for grand piano rims, and a few makes have rims made of spruce, the same material used for the sound-board.

THE KEYBOARD

Most uprights and grand pianos have a keyboard with eighty-eight keys. Older models sometimes have three fewer at the high end, while Bösendorfer produce large grands with four or even nine extra keys in the bass register. The extra-long strings for these keys also contribute a certain richness to the tone of the instrument.

Ivory or synthetic

In the past, the white keys were almost always covered with ivory, but trade in ivory has been prohibited since 1989. The synthetic *key covering* that is now in general use feels a little smoother than ivory, but it discolours less quickly and is easier to maintain. Some brands use imitation ivory, given names like *ivoplast* or *ivorite.* Other manufacturers cover the keys of some models with bone or mammoth ivory, taken from the bodies of mammoths, preserved under the Siberian ice for thousands of years.

Ebony or plastic

The black keys are usually made of a type of plastic. Only more expensive models and older instruments still have black keys made of wood, usually ebony. Many pianists prefer wood to plastics because they say it feels better – it isn't as smooth or slippery.

Balanced

The keys must be well balanced. If a key is too light on the side which is fingered, it will be hard work to play – and if it is too heavy the touch will be too light. In order to balance the keys properly, small pieces of *key lead* are set into them. In uprights they are often placed near the ends of the keys, where they are invisible from the outside. If they are set into the side of the keys, as in grand pianos, you can sometimes just about see them if you press down the neighbouring keys completely.

Key dip

In a well-regulated grand piano, the keys can be pressed down about 0.4" (1cm). If this depth or key dip is too big, it takes too long before the instrument responds, which makes it hard to play rapid passages. If the key dip is too small, the difference between loud and soft becomes very small. The key dip has to be the same for each key. In factories, this is – or is supposed to be – regulated to the nearest tenth of a millimetre.

Equally high and evenly spaced

On used instruments especially, it's a good idea to check whether all the keys are at the same height (usually a matter of proper regulation) and whether the gaps between keys are equally wide all the way along the keyboard. The keys should not touch each other at any point.

Long keys, short keys

The keys of a grand piano are slightly longer than those of an upright, which is one of the reasons why a grand feels different when it's played, as the longer keys give you more control over the tone. It's hard work playing very short keys, such as you sometimes find on very small pianos. The smaller action plays a role too.

Keyboard

Most piano manufacturers buy in quite a lot of their components. There are specialist factories for all kinds of parts, as you will see later in this chapter. Kluge and Langer, for instance, are the two best-known keyboard makers. Some piano manufacturers buy all their keyboards from these firms, others use them only for their top models.

Does better-known mean better?

Two tips: most manufacturers won't use expensive parts by famous makes in a piano that isn't really worth it. On the other hand, a list of prestigious brand names doesn't necessarily mean a piano will sound great.

THE ACTION

When you press down a key and then release it, you set a whole series of parts in motion. The mechanism, or action, only works well if the whole instrument is properly regulated.

Loads

Each key has an action made up of some sixty or seventy parts, including the *front-rail pin*, the *damper-spring bushing* and the *whippen-flange screw*. Exactly what all of those parts do is described in countless books on the technical side of the piano.

Simultaneously

The action is as complicated as it is because all kinds of things have to happen simultaneously or in quick succession. Hammer to string, damper off, hammer straight back and ready for the next note, damper back, and so on.

Quality

A piano with a better action plays better, feels better and lasts longer. Of course, even the best action won't feel good if it isn't properly regulated.

Set-off

One example: if you look inside a piano and at the same time very slowly press down a key, you'll see that the hammer falls back just before it touches the string. This is called the *set-off* or *escapement*, which is controlled by the *set-off* button. If the set-off is too big, the hammer falls back too soon: in that case, you won't make any sound at all if you play very softly, playing loudly becomes difficult, and just producing a decent-sounding note is tricky. If it is too small, there's a chance that the hammer will hit the string twice when you play softly: this is called *double-striking*.

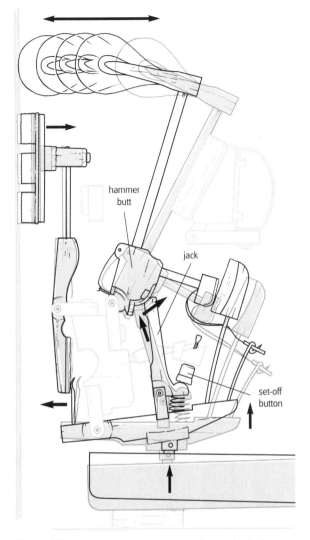

The set-off button sets when the jack escapes from under the hammer butt so that the hammer can fall back.

Not all the same

Every instrument 'feels' different, one a bit lighter, the next a bit heavier or more solid. This mainly reflects the force you need to press the keys down and the force they come back up with (the *up weight*). One advantage of having a good ratio between the two is that you can play repeated notes more rapidly.

Touch weight

If you like a solid-feeling keyboard, you're probably more likely to choose an instrument with a fairly high *touch weight*. The touch weight is a combination of the up weight and the *down weight* (the force needed to play a soft note). The down weight usually varies between 1.6 and 1.95 ounces (45–55 grams) and the up weight between 0.7 and 1.05 ounces (20–30 grams).

A tip: just sitting down and playing will usually tell you more than those figures ever will. Some brochures mention them – but most don't.

Lighter or heavier

A piano with keys that have a heavy touch, or are hard work to play, can be regulated to make them a bit lighter – and the other way around – but there are limits. The correct regulation depends on things like the type of action and the way the rest of the instrument is built.

Further up the key

You can best tell how hard or light the touch of a piano is by playing fast passages. You'll also feel the difference if you play with your fingers further towards the back of the keys. Some chords and fingerings require you to do this anyway.

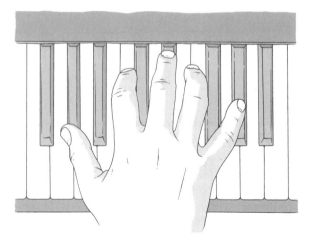

An A-flat major chord: you feel the difference more easily further up the key

Even

All keys must feel the same. Play fast and play slowly, play loud and play softly, and use the whole keyboard. The better your playing, the more likely you are to sense how even and how good everything feels. If you are a beginner, take someone along who can play well for advice.

Unresponsive

Some keyboards can be very slow to respond: press down a key and there is a short delay before anything happens. They also give you little control over the tone, and the dynamic range (from loud to soft) is very small. That can be a question of poor regulation but – on used instruments – it can also be a sign of wear.

Regulate first

If you have your eye on a piano but the feel isn't ideal and you think regulation will do the trick, then have it regulated, and play it again before you buy the instrument.

Who needs a good action?

Do you only need a really good action if you are a good pianist? No. Even if you have just started, your playing will feel better on a good, properly-regulated action – so you'll probably play longer and enjoy it more. Once again: if a piano is only 'good enough to start on', you may not get much further than starting.

Fast and responsive

On a grand piano, the hammers and the dampers simply drop back into place when you let go of the keys. That's one of the reasons why a grand piano action feels more responsive and gives you more control over the tone and the dynamics – and why you can repeat notes more quickly on it (up to twelve times a second). A grand piano key doesn't have to come right back up before you can hit it again. An upright key does have to.

Repetition mechanism

That's why you can't repeat a note more than eight or nine times a second on most uprights, assuming your technique allows you to play that fast. However, various manufacturers have devised systems to get round the problem. Such

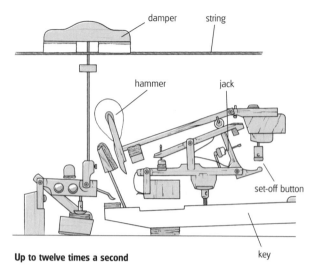

damper   string
hammer   jack
set-off button
Up to twelve times a second   key

systems may use a special repetition lever (Steingraeber), a
set of magnets (SMR, a Dutch invention used by Seiler) or
a spring (Sauter's R2 system or Fandrich's Vertical Action).
They are standard on some makes and optional on others
– if optional, you will pay more for a piano with the system
installed. Repeater systems usually demand very precise
regulation and they can be more sensitive to changes in
humidity (see page 94 and onwards). You won't find them
in the lowest or highest price ranges.

Faster
Even without those systems, one piano may repeat faster
than the next. How far the keys have to come back up
before you can use them again may give you an indication
of how fast an instrument can be played.

All the keys
If you have found an instrument that sounds good and
feels good to play, try the keys one by one. Play them equally
hard and listen for rattles or buzzes, check that each note
sounds equally loud and that the dampers mute each one
equally quickly and evenly. Remember, the highest fifteen
to twenty notes don't have dampers (see page 50).

Tricky legato
Dampers mustn't leave the string too late, but they must not

return too quickly either. If strings get muted again too soon, it is very hard to play a proper legato, when each note has to flow smoothly into the next.

Wood or synthetic?

Synthetic action parts are quite widely used, especially in the lower price ranges. Modern varieties are better suited to the job than the synthetics used in the Sixties, which tended to become brittle. That's something you need to check, or have checked, if you intend to buy a piano made in that period.

Brands

Actions are often built by specialized manufacturers too, usually according to the specifications of the piano manufacturer. The best-known maker of actions is Renner. Other names include Defil, Langer, Pratt-Win and Tofa.

HAMMERS AND DAMPERS

For a piano to sound good it has to have good hammer heads and all the hammers must be precisely regulated. The same is true for the dampers.

Large heads

Large and heavy hammer heads are needed to set the long and thick bass strings in motion. Big heavy dampers are needed to mute them again properly. The higher-sounding the string, the smaller the hammer head used, and the dampers, too, get smaller and smaller as you move up the keyboard.

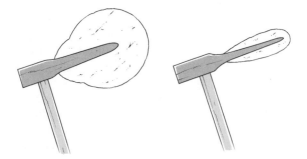

A hammer head for a bass string, and one for a high treble string

No dampers

The strings of the highest one-and-a-half octaves vibrate so briefly that they don't need a damper at all. On most pianos, the last damper is somewhere between e3 and a3 (see page 13). The first key without a damper is often easy to find just by ear: simply play short notes in an ascending scale until you hear the first note that goes on sounding when you release the key.

As small as possible

That transition must not be too big, but you will always hear the difference. To make it as small as possible, most instruments are regulated so that the last damper only mutes very slightly.

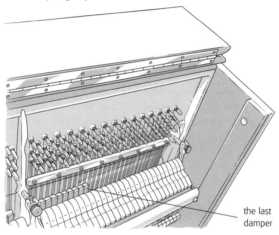

the last damper

The highest-sounding strings don't need dampers

Just as high, just as far

On a well-regulated piano, the hammers are all at the same position along the strings: if a hammer strikes a string too high up or too low down, that note will sound noticeably different to the rest – especially with the high notes. All hammers should also be equally far from the strings.

Stuck

The space between two hammers must always be equally wide. If hammers are too close together or do not move in a straight line, there's a chance that they will touch or even jam when you are playing. And of course, if one of the hammers is crooked and doesn't strike its string(s) properly, that note won't sound as good.

Extra string

On very small uprights a hammer may graze a string from the next unison along. You'll only hear it if the dampers are off (press the right-hand pedal down) and if you listen well.

Voicing

The hammer heads must have the correct hardness if they are to produce a good tone. If necessary, they can be softened by pricking them with needles. The process of *voicing* or *toning* is usually done in the factory, although some piano shops revoice the instruments themselves.

You can only adjust so far

So, by having a piano voiced, you can adjust its tone. If the hammer heads are made slightly harder, the tone becomes brighter, while softer heads give a warmer tone. On the other hand, of course, it's not just the hammer heads which determine the tone. That means there is a limit to the degree that voicing can change an instrument's tone. To read more about hammer heads and voicing, turn to the secondhand buying tips on page 67 and chapter 10 on tuning and regulation (page 105).

Shrill

Voicing takes time. On cheap instruments especially, the tone can sometimes become noticeably harsher or shriller after just a few months because the hammer heads have not been properly voiced. Ultimately, every piano needs to be revoiced.

Heavy felt

Some brochures mention exactly how heavy the felt of the hammer heads is. Taken on their own, such figures once again tell you little: the 'best' felt weight depends very much on the design of the whole instrument.

Brands

Abel and Renner are two well-known manufacturers of hammer heads.

STRINGS

Both uprights and grand pianos have around two hundred and twenty strings. At first sight, there's nothing much to check for in those strings, except to ensure that they are evenly spaced as they run across the instrument – but there is more to see and to know than that.

Twenty-five feet

Of the thinnest, highest strings, usually only a section of two or three inches (5–8cm) actually vibrates. If the longest bass string were equally thick, it would need to be a good twenty, twenty-five feet (7–8m) to sound as low as it does.

Wound strings

Obviously that wouldn't be practical. To get round this problem, you can make the strings a good deal thicker, allowing them to sound lower without becoming too long. For this reason, all bass strings are wound with copper wire: the lowest string even has two or three layers.

Single, double and triple strings

The very lowest notes have only one string each. The higher-sounding bass notes are double-strung unisons: each hammer strikes two strings at once. In the treble area there are three plain, non-wound steel strings for each note.

Transition

As you move from the bass strings to the low treble three things change: the lower treble strings run across a different bridge, they are not wound and there are three of them for each note. You'd expect to be able to hear a transition like that very clearly. To make this transition as smooth as possible, the low treble section often starts with a few double, wound string unisons.

Listen

In other words, on a good, properly voiced piano, the transition will be as small as possible. That means no note sounds noticeably fuller, less bright or more metallic than the one next to it. A tip for when you're listening: play near the transition, note by note, very softly. Don't look at the strings. If you do, you may end up only seeing the difference instead of hearing it.

Scale

The word *scale* may refer to only the *speaking length* of the strings (the part that vibrates), but often it is also used to mean the precise number, thickness and the winding of the strings and everything directly connected with these things. In a piano featuring a *German scale design* the stringing is based on a German model – which of course tells you nothing about the quality of the instrument. The picture below shows roughly how the strings are grouped.

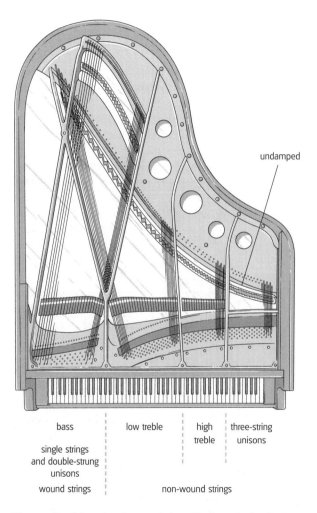

undamped

bass	low treble	high treble	three-string unisons
single strings and double-strung unisons			
wound strings	non-wound strings		

The grouping of the strings in a grand piano. The layout is virtually the same in an upright.

Smaller piano, thicker strings

The smaller a piano is, the thicker the strings need to be if they are to be tuned low enough. That's one of the reasons why small pianos often sound less rich or full than tall instruments of the same quality: the thicker a string is, the stiffer it gets, and a stiff, short string is harder to set in motion than a long thin one. On very small pianos with poor quality strings some notes can sound very shrill and even slightly out of tune, even if the instrument is properly tuned. It's a result of the excessive stiffness of the strings.

The best?

It's not a simple matter to judge the quality of the strings. Nor is it easy to fit another set of strings, as you might with a guitar. You can assume that a decent piano will have decent strings, and that barring exceptional circumstances, those strings will last for half a century.

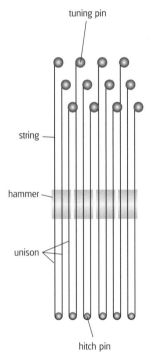

Loop-strung unisons: each section of string serves as two strings

Replacing strings

If you really want to get the best from your instrument you might consider having the strings replaced after about twenty or thirty years, when they have lost some of their tone and brightness. Grand pianos in concert halls have their strings replaced much more frequently.

Loop strung

The three-string unisons are usually *loop strung*: one long section of a string is fixed to a tuning-pin, looped around the hitch-pin and then fixed again to the neighbouring tuning-pin. In other words, a single length of string serves as two strings.

Single stringing

Very few makes have three separate strings for a three-string unison, and those that do are expensive. This is fairly easy to check on an open grand piano: if it has separate strings, each one is tied to the hitch-pin. The technical term is *single stringing*. Bass strings are always fixed in this way.

Round or octagonal

The steel strings are just about always made in specialist factories. Well-known makes include Giese, Mapes, Poehlman and Röslau. However, winding the bass strings is a job piano manufacturers often do themselves. The cores of wound strings are sometimes six or eight-sided, something that can be seen and felt along the unwound parts of those strings. Cores like this make the winding easier and keep the windings in place better, at least according to some specialists. Others say that a round core gives a more solid tone. You find both types in both the most expensive and cheaper instruments, and in the end it's how the whole instrument sounds that counts.

From thick to thin

To give you an idea: the thickest strings are at least six or seven times as thick as the thinnest, and the sounding part can be twenty or thirty times as long.

Tension

The amount of tension on the strings varies with the make. It's affected by the construction of the instrument, the choice of strings, and most of all by the views of the manufacturer. For instance, a lower string tension is said by some to give a more singing and longer tone, and a high tension a brighter tone. Some manufacturers believe that a string will sound at its best if it is tightened to the verge of breaking. Others disagree.

PINS, BLOCKS AND BRIDGES

The strings run from the tuning-pins to the hitch-pins. On the way they pass over the bridge, which transmits the vibrations to the soundboard, and also the pressure bar, or a number of agraffes, and sometimes a set of small metal combs.

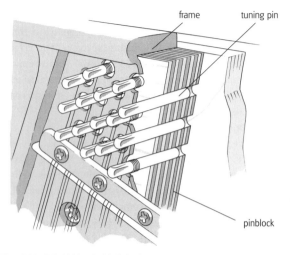

frame   tuning pin

pinblock

The pinblock is hidden behind the frame

Pinblock

The pinblock, holding the tuning-pins, has to withstand a great deal of pressure, which is why it's made up of a number of layers of hardwood, sometimes three, sometimes thirty or more. You'll come across all the variations on both expensive and cheap makes: the number of layers doesn't say a thing about the quality of the block or the instrument.

Makes

Well-known pinblock manufacturers are Delignit and Dehonit, both from Germany. There are also piano manufacturers who make their own pinblocks.

Slightly upwards

In order to withstand the tension of the strings, the tuning-pins in an upright piano usually point slightly upwards. In a grand piano they point slightly towards the player. There must be some space between the string and the frame, otherwise it would be impossible to further tighten the string should it be necessary. This space also means that if a tuning-pin comes slightly loose over the course of many years it can be hammered a bit deeper into the pinblock.

The same angle

If all the tuning-pins are not set at the same angle, or if some pins are obviously deeper than others, something is

wrong with the pinblock. And on a well-constructed piano
the tuning-pins are set far enough apart for the strings not
to touch each other at any point.

Bridges

A violin has a small, thin wooden bridge that transmits the
vibrations of the strings to the body, which amplifies
them. Pianos actually work in just the same way: two
bridges pass on the vibrations to the soundboard, which
amplifies the sound. There is a short bridge for the bass
strings and a long one for the rest.

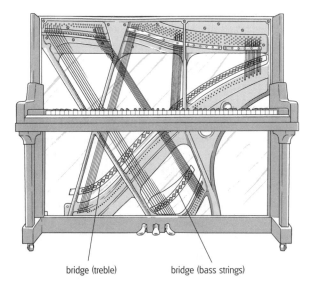

bridge (treble)   bridge (bass strings)

The bridges transmit the vibrations of the strings to the soundboard...

bridge

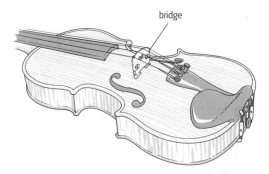

... just as a violin bridge transmits the vibrations of the strings to the body.

Bridge pins

The better the contact between bridge and strings, the better the vibrations are transmitted. That's why the strings run zigzag across the bridge, kept in place by the *bridge pins*. These small metal pins also help to transmit the vibrations.

Pressure bar

From the tuning-pins the strings either run under a metal bar, or through small brass blocks. The *pressure bar* keeps the strings in place by pressing them with great force against one of the edges of the frame, and the brass blocks (*agraffes*) do the same. Because these agraffes have one hole for each string, the strings are automatically spaced at the right distance from each other – which is convenient for whoever has to fit the strings.

Agraffes

Almost all grand pianos have agraffes for the bass strings and the low treble, and a pressure bar or *capo d'astro* for the high treble. On upright pianos you find almost all possible combinations in almost all price ranges. Agraffes throughout, a pressure bar for all the strings, or perhaps agraffes only for the bass strings. In other words, the use of agraffes or pressure bars says nothing about the quality or price.

agraffes   pressure bar

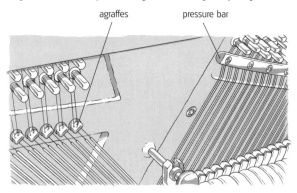

Agraffes for the bass strings, a pressure bar for the higher-sounding strings

The ends

The ends of the strings, the parts near the tuning-pins at one end and the hitch-pins at the other, do not belong to the speaking length of the string. Even so, they do vibrate very softly in sympathy. That can be disturbing, especially on the lower strings, which is why a strip of felt is often threaded between the ends of those strings.

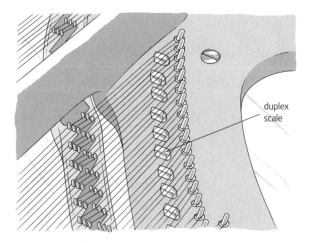

A duplex scale with small adjustable combs for each unison (Estonia)

Duplex scale

In many grand pianos, the end parts of the higher-sounding strings are used to make the tone richer: with the help of special small bridges, these short sections of the strings are tuned so that they resonate with the speaking lengths of the strings. This system, known as the *duplex scale*, was invented by Steinway.

Duller

You can easily hear how important those vibrations at the ends of the strings are by putting a finger on one and playing the appropriate key. You'll find that the tone is noticeably duller.

Aliquot scale

There is another method used to give the highest octaves a richer sound: all the three-string unisons have a fourth string added. This string is not struck by the hammer, but resonates if you play quite loudly. This system is mainly found on Blüthner pianos: its name, *aliquot scale*, comes from the French *son aliquot*, meaning a harmonic.

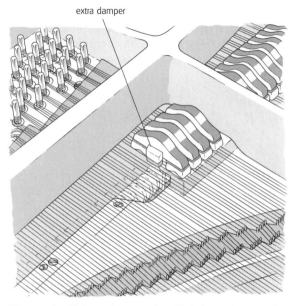

extra damper

Aliquot scale with four strings per unison. Each damper has a small extra damper attached for the fourth string (Blüthner)

SOUNDBOARD

The soundboard is often referred to as the soul or the voice of the instrument. Usually, this large wooden plate is made up of thin planks of spruce. It is no coincidence that this is the same type of wood used for the tops of violin and guitar bodies. Soundboards come in varying qualities.

Grain

The vibrations need to be able to pass through the whole soundboard very quickly if they are to produce a good tone. Vibrations move fastest if the wood has a straight, fine grain. This type of grain is found especially in wood from Alaska, Siberia and other cold regions, because the trees there grow very slowly.

Crown

The soundboard isn't flat: in a grand piano the centre rises about a third of an inch (1cm). In an upright, the soundboard curves towards the player. This curve, called the *crown* or *belly*, keeps the wood under tension and contributes to the tone.

Ribs

The *ribs* or *barring* at the back (or on a grand, the bottom) of the soundboard are perpendicular to the grain of the wood. This allows them to help distribute the vibrations across the soundboard faster. They also help keep the soundboard in shape.

A bit flatter

After many years, most soundboards do get a bit flatter, and that makes the tone a bit flatter too. On the other hand, however important a crown is, there are plenty of instruments old and new which sound excellent but have no crown at all or one which is barely visible.

Cracks

The forces on the soundboard can not only flatten it in time, but can also cause cracks. These can occur very rapidly if the wood shrinks or expands a lot, for instance if it is exposed to rapid swings in temperature or humidity. Eventually, after half a century or more, just about every soundboard will develop cracks. Fortunately, not all cracks are too serious. You can read more about avoiding cracks, having them repaired and about how serious they are on page 69, and on page 94 and onwards.

From thick to thin

Most soundboards are about one-third of an inch (1cm) thick at the high treble end, with a very fine grain: this increases its stiffness, which helps give a decent sound to even the highest strings. At the bass end the soundboard is often a little thinner and has a coarser grain, enhancing the lower frequencies. All kinds of ideas have been dreamt up to help soundboards to 'sing'. For instance, there are soundboards with a groove around them, which supposedly allows them to vibrate more freely.

Bigger? Maybe not

One of the reasons that larger instruments have a 'bigger' sound is because they have a larger soundboard. You can't always tell the size of the soundboard from the outside, as sometimes the cabinet of an upright is taller than usual but the soundboard is no bigger than the average. On the other hand, some manufacturers produce extra wide grand pianos. These do have bigger soundboards than equally long grand pianos of a different brand.

Laminated soundboards

Some cheaper uprights have a laminated soundboard made up of thin layers of wood rather than solid planks. A laminated soundboard is more resistant to changes in humidity and temperature than a solid soundboard.

Not top quality

The earliest laminated soundboards were mostly used in pianos that were very cheap and not especially good. These days instruments with laminated soundboards can be well built and sound good. Still, you won't find this type of soundboard in the very best instruments: a good solid soundboard contributes to a richer tone.

How to tell

If you look at a laminated soundboard, you'll notice the grain at the back of the soundboard is different to the grain you see from the inside. Another clue is that the grain runs straight down instead of diagonally. If there is a hole in the soundboard, you can see whether the wood is layered or solid by examining the edges of the hole.

PEDALS

Most uprights and grand pianos have three pedals. Only the right-hand pedal has the same function on both instruments.

Right-hand pedal

The right-hand pedal is called the *damper pedal* (because it moves all the dampers away from the strings), or *sustain* or *sustaining pedal* (because moving the dampers away allows the strings to sustain their notes). It is commonly referred to as the right pedal or the 'loud pedal'.

Different sound

The sound changes when you use this pedal too: the strings of the keys you don't play vibrate along softly with everything you do play. Play the chord shown opposite and keep the keys pressed down a little while. Let them go.

Now press down the right pedal, play the same chord, and hear the difference.

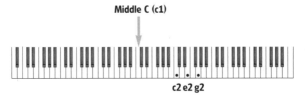

Middle C (c1)

c2 e2 g2

Play long notes: first without, then with the right pedal

At the same time

When you press the pedal down, try to see whether all the dampers leave the strings at the same time. If you use this pedal a lot, you're likely to keep your foot resting on it lightly. For this reason, the dampers shouldn't respond to that very light pressure, but only move when you press the pedal down a little further. A good pedal allows you to control the dampers very precisely, moving them to and from the strings as fast or as slowly as the music requires.

Rattles and buzzes

You should also listen for any unwanted extra noises when testing the pedals. For example, play a chord loudly with the right-hand pedal pressed down, and then let the pedal come back up very slowly. Are all the notes damped equally and at the same time? Are there any rattles, buzzes or squeaks?

Left-hand pedal

If you press down the left-hand pedal of an upright piano, the hammers move closer to the strings. This means they don't travel as far before striking the strings, which reduces the volume. This pedal is known as the *left*, *soft* or *piano pedal* (from the Italian *piano*, 'soft'). Grand pianos have a different way of attaining a similar effect, as described below.

A different feel

If you use the left pedal, the action feels slightly different. This is because, since the hammers move forwards slightly, a tiny bit of space opens up above the jack (see page 45): so the jack travels through the air for a very short distance before it strikes the hammer and sends it toward the string. This bit of 'air' can make the keyboard feel unresponsive and slightly uneven, and it also gives you a little less control over the tone. The effect is more marked on some pianos than on others.

The middle pedal

The middle pedal can be used to operate various quite different mechanisms and effects. On many uprights, it's a *practice pedal*. When you press it down you lower a strip of felt between the hammers and the strings, which is nice for the neighbours: it substantially reduces the volume. Unfortunately, it also makes the piano feel quite different.

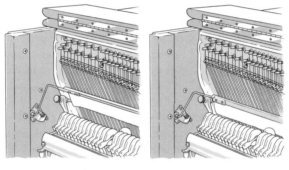

not muted   muted

A strip of felt between hammers and strings

Locked

Most practice pedals can be locked into the 'on' position, either by moving it a little to the left when you press it down, or by simply pressing it down once (in this case the pedal comes back up when you press it a second time).

By hand

The felt strip, known as a *moderator* or *moderator stop*, can also be operated with a handle instead of a pedal. The handle is usually under the keyboard. The most basic versions of all require you to open the lid before you can lower or raise the felt.

Bass sustain

On other uprights, especially American-made ones, the

middle pedal is a bass sustain pedal, which lifts the dampers of the bass strings alone. This is only really useful if all the notes you want to sustain are in that part of the register.

Muting system
Sometimes the middle pedal is used to activate a muting system. With the muting system switched on the hammers no longer touch the strings, and you need a pair of headphones to hear yourself play. On other models you operate the muting system with a handle under the keyboard. Many pianos with a muting system don't have a moderator stop, and some models have both. You can read more about pianos with muting systems in chapter 7.

Purely decorative
Do note: on some cheaper pianos the third pedal is purely decorative – either it does nothing at all, or it does the same as the left-hand pedal.

Optional extra
If the piano you are planning to buy has no moderator, you may be able to have one installed. It'll cost somewhere between £150 and £500/$250 and $750, depending on the make of piano. Hand-operated models are cheaper. Grand pianos very rarely have such a mechanism.

Grands and lyres
The lyre is the part of a grand piano that holds the pedals. On some grands it still has a lyre shape.

Not just softer...
When you press down the *una corda* pedal (left-hand pedal) of a grand piano, the sound is quieter because one fewer string is struck in each unison. But that isn't all.

... but milder too
In the normal position, when the strings are struck by the

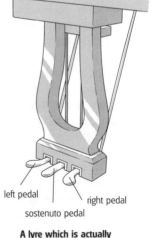

left pedal
right pedal
sostenuto pedal

A lyre which is actually shaped like a lyre

hammers, they compress the felt into grooves, and the felt in these grooves is a little harder than the rest of the hammer. If you now press down the left pedal, the strings are struck by the softer part of the hammer, just beside those grooves. This changes the tone as well as the volume: milder, softer and more nasal are often used descriptions.

One out of two strings

The term *una corda* originated in the eighteenth century. Early grands had two strings for each note: of those two, only one was struck if you played una corda: una corda is Italian for 'one string'. Incidentally, in those days the system wasn't operated by means of a pedal.

One less, one more

When you press the una corda pedal, the hammers should move far enough to the side to strike one fewer string in each unison, but not so far as to graze one of the strings in the next unison.

If you hear strange singing noises when you use the pedal this may indicate that the action is being moved too far. If you press down the keys very slowly one by one, you can clearly see whether the hammers are striking where they should.

Sostenuto pedal

Nearly all modern grand pianos have a sostenuto pedal; many older models don't. Does that matter? There isn't a lot of music that absolutely requires this third grand piano pedal. It is sometimes called a *Steinway pedal*, because this make acquired the patent to the original sostenuto pedal invented by Pleyel in 1875.

And very occasionally

Some pianos can be ordered with a sostenuto pedal for an extra £200/$750 or more. On old instruments you may come across a *bass sostenuto*: in other words, the pedal only works for the bass register. Another unusual variation, but this time a new one: the Italian brand Fazioli makes grands with a fourth pedal, which works in a similar way to the left-hand pedal of an upright piano. It doesn't, however, have the disadvantages that this pedal on an upright has (see page 63).

SECONDHAND

As a non-professional you can't really judge a secondhand piano properly – certainly not if it's an older instrument in somebody's home. Even so, there are all kinds of things you can check for yourself, as well as everything you've read about above. And if you like the look of an instrument, you can always have it valued (see page 23).

Play, look and listen

When you are playing, listen out for rattles or buzzes, watch out for keys which are hard work to play, creak or squeak, and for hammers which double-strike when you play softly. Check that there are no keys that can move to the left or right too easily. The greatest wear is usually in the middle part of the keyboard: that's where pianos get played the most.

Very light

If a piano has a very light feel there is often 'air' or lost motion in the action. It's often very hard or impossible to play a piano like this really softly, the volume is very difficult to control and often you'll hear all kinds of noises.

Inside

Take a look inside as well. Ask the person selling the piano to remove lamps, vases or anything else from the instrument, and ask them to open the lid: that will avoid problems with falling objects, breakages and the like.

Hammers

Check whether all the hammers are in the right place (see page 50). Hold down different groups of keys and look to see whether the hammers are still in line. When you let them go, the hammers should all fall back at the same time.

Heads with grooves

Grooves in the hammer heads are normal on a used piano. Look especially carefully at the hammer heads in the middle section: they usually have the most to put up with. The grooves should never be too near the edge of the head, but roughly in the middle. The strings should also fall exactly into those grooves: you can check that by pressing the keys down very softly.

Deep grooves and moths

If the grooves are very deep, the hammer heads can be sanded back into shape if the felt is still thick enough, and if it hasn't dried out too much. Take another look at the hammers: moths have a taste for felt. If you need new hammer heads you can expect to pay £400/$600 or more.

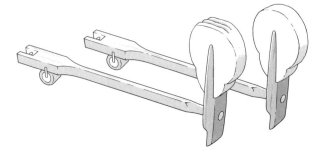

A worn-out hammer head with deep grooves, and a new head

Strings

If the instrument has rusty strings it may have been standing in a very damp place. That can be a problem if you move it to a house with central heating and air conditioning (see page 94). Rust also dulls the tone, and rusty strings are harder to tune. If you find new strings among a set of mostly old ones, it can be a sign that more strings are likely to break.

Properly tuned

You can only judge a piano if it's properly tuned, whether it's secondhand or new. If a piano is a good deal too low over the whole range, it won't sound out of tune – but it will be a problem if you want to play with others. Besides, a piano sounds best when tuned to the right pitch. Last but not least, a piano which sounds a semitone or more too low usually can't be tuned to pitch with a single tuning. So how can you check the pitch?

Tuning fork

For about £3/$5 you can buy a tuning fork that produces the A that most instruments tune to, although a more expensive model will be more reliable. The fork will be labelled A=440 (see page 103). On a piano this is a1, the A slightly to the right of the centre. Tap the tuning fork against your knee or a hard surface and hold the stem against the cabinet or close to your ear. If key and tuning fork sound exactly the same, then the piano is at the right pitch. If the A-sharp/B-flat (the black key to the right of the A) is at the same pitch as the tuning fork, the piano is tuned a semitone too low.

With a tuning fork you can check whether a piano is tuned too low or too high

Tuner
You could also take an electronic tuner with you. Most guitarists and bassists have one. A device like this allows you to see at a glance whether the piano is at the right pitch.

Cracks
Large cracks in the soundboard are easy to see, but you'll need an expert to spot smaller cracks. This is especially true when you're inspecting the crown. Non-professionals can't judge parts like the pinblock and the bridges properly either. Do check that the tuning-pins are all at the same angle, that the ribs are still touching the soundboard all along their length, and that they are not cracked. It's worth knowing that replacing or repairing a soundboard can easily cost more than a decent new piano. If the panels look crooked there's a good chance that the soundboard is no longer in shape either.

Woodworm
Holes in the wood could mean that the piano is infested with woodworm. Woodworm don't like music, so if a piano has been played frequently it's probably not inhabited.

Overdamper
If you come across a piano that has dampers above the hammers, you can assume it's probably over a hundred years old. This type of piano (an *overdamper*) is not usually worth much.

Straight-strung

Another type to be wary of is the straight-strung piano, on which the strings run vertically. They are usually very old and not usually worth a great deal. However, a decent model can fetch £600–700/$900–1100. Note that the Dutch firm Rippen was still building straight-strung instruments up until the 1980s.

Age

If you want to know exactly how old an instrument is you can find tables with serial numbers and year of build for nearly all makes in the *Pierce Piano Atlas* and similar books. Many piano shops have a copy you can browse through. You can find lists like this on the Internet too (see page 135). The serial number is often shown on the frame, but sometimes it's under the lid, on the pinblock or on the soundboard. A tip: some components have their own individual numbers, so don't mistake these for the serial number.

6. PLAYING AND LISTENING

This chapter contains tips for playing and listening to supplement the previous chapter: about playing yourself, even if you can't really play yet, to help you hear the difference between one instrument and the next, and to guide you towards a better understanding of what you do hear.

In a shop, everything sounds different from how it will at home. If you ask the salesperson to first let you hear a very bright sounding piano, and then a very 'warm' one, you'll get an idea of the acoustics of the room you're in, and of how various different instruments sound in it. Thinking about the price is not the point right now.

Start with the extremes

These two extremes are also a good starting point if you don't yet have a clear idea of which sound you want. Decide which of the two appeals to you most, and carry on looking from there.

Another tip: you can also play (or get someone to play) the cheapest and the most expensive piano in the shop right after each other, or one model from each price range. That may give you a better picture of the differences between instruments related to price, and what you can and should listen out for.

Your own piano

Another starting point is, of course, the instrument you already have – if you do already have one. Some piano salespeople will even visit your home: that gives them an idea of the room where the instrument will be played and of the character (and the trade-in value) of the instrument you are currently playing.

Loud or soft

An instrument sounds much louder, brighter and more direct in a room with hard acoustics (wooden floor, no curtains, little furniture) than in a room with thick rugs and carpets. You need to take that into account when making a choice. The tone can be adjusted slightly (*voicing*, see page 51), but if you want to give a piano with a decidedly bright tone a very warm, romantic character, you are likely to be disappointed.

Impressive

Many piano shops have quite hard acoustics. That means almost any instrument will sound impressive if you are a half-decent pianist, you press down the right-hand pedal and open the lid wide.

Someone else

Just about every piano salesperson knows how to play the instrument. Even so, if you haven't been playing very long yourself, it can be a good idea to take another pianist along. Preferably one who can play what you would like to play yourself and most importantly someone who will show you what the *piano* can do rather than what *they* can do.

Quite wrong

Even if you do play, having a second pianist along can't do any harm. Then you can get the other person to play, so that you can listen better. Or you can let that other person play without you seeing which instrument they are playing – and you may find you are quite wrong about which piano you think you are listening to.

Comparisons

Choosing instruments by their tone and timbre is primarily a question of making comparisons. The first piano you play may sound great – but often you'll only really be able to judge if you play a couple of other instruments immediately afterwards.

At home

If you are buying at somebody's home, there's nothing to compare the piano with, which makes it even more important to take someone along who can play if you don't (yet) play yourself. They can help you judge not only how the instrument sounds, but also how it plays.

PLAYING

If you sit down to play in a shop, try not to wonder what the salesperson thinks of your playing. They shouldn't be listening to how you play but to what you play, in order to help in choosing an instrument that suits you.

Briefly

If you have a lot of pianos to choose from, it may be best to start by playing each instrument only briefly. Once you have narrowed down your choice to a manageable number, compare them two by two or three by three. Discard the one you like least and choose another in its place. And so on. Naturally, once you've narrowed down the field you will want to play for longer.

Simple

To start with, play simple things – otherwise you'll be concentrating more on playing than on listening. Just scales and chords will help you form a first impression.

Even if you can't play

The chords shown on the following page will give you a fair impression of how a piano sounds. Even if you don't play properly yet, you can manage these: after all, playing a chord is no more than playing a few keys at the same time. To begin with, choose one of the three chords and play only the keys with the black dots. If you have been playing for longer, then play the keys with the grey dots too. These three chords will sound best in the order shown if you play them one after the other.

Long notes

Very short notes tell you less about the tone of an instrument than long notes. So keep the keys pressed down while you listen.

D minor chord (D minor 7)

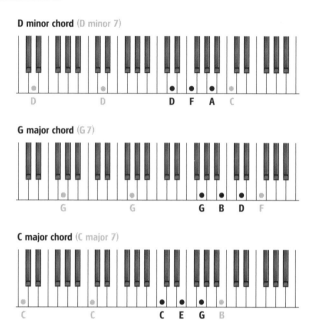

D   D   **D** **F** **A** C

G major chord (G 7)

G   G   **G** **B** **D** F

C major chord (C major 7)

C   C   **C** **E** **G** B

Three useful chords for testing. You can play only the keys with the black dots, or include the other keys as well.

High, middle and low

Another simple playing and listening tip is to play the same three-note chord at different places on the keyboard.

Middle C (c1)

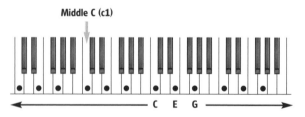

C **E** **G**

The same chord, played along the whole keyboard (C major)

Same chord, different instrument

You can also try playing the same chord in the same register on different pianos. If you try putting what you hear into words, the differences may be easier to remember. Think of words like velvety or bright, warm or full, nasal, rich, thin or shrill – or think in colours: one piano may sound 'yellower' than another to you.

Colour

Pianists often talk about colour in a different way too: the better the instrument is the more 'colours' you can get out of it, provided you can play well enough.

Play longer

You'll naturally want to play longer on those instruments from which you are going to make your final choice. Listening is easiest if you play pieces you know well. And play all kinds of things, from loud to soft, with and without pedals, and from as fast as you can to notes that last a minute each.

Empty music stands

If you are used to playing from sheet music, take your books with you when you go to choose a piano. Playing can suddenly seem very difficult with an empty music stand.

LISTENING

You can't learn how to listen just by reading about it, but you can read about what to listen out for.

Even progression

Of course the high notes on a piano always sound different than the low notes, but the progression should be very even. Nor should the transitions be too large, for instance when moving from the bass notes to the low treble (page 52), or from damped to undamped high notes (page 50).

Soft and loud

On a good piano you can play very softly and still depend on every note. You should also be able to play very loudly without the sound distorting or becoming too shrill, or the notes merging together so that no one can hear what you are playing. An instrument that can do all this has good dynamics.

Louder and brighter

As you start playing with more force, the instrument not only starts to sound louder, but brighter too. This is something else to listen out for, because the degree and evenness of that change is different on different instruments.

Try a grand too

Grand pianos generally have a bigger dynamic range than uprights. Even if you are after an upright try listening to what a good grand piano can do, just so you know what's possible.

A bigger dynamic range

The lower notes

The differences in character between different uprights or grands often come out best when you play the lower notes, in the area from the first to the third octave. Keep playing the same chord or passage in the same octave, equally loudly or softly, on different instruments.

Every note

Check that every note remains audible in the very lowest register, even if you play two in very quick succession or at the same time. You should also be able to hear the difference between notes clearly when you start from the very lowest and go up slowly, note by note. Another two tips: in a good instrument you can almost feel the bass notes, and a good low note doesn't drone – it sounds.

High

The highest notes always sound short, but they should still sing. A 'plink' is not enough. Go up note by note in the high register and ask yourself whether you can always hear a clear difference from the previous note.

Middle

The low treble is perhaps the area in which pianos resemble one another the most. It's also the area where you'll play most often. But when you're really playing, you'll certainly hear the difference between one instrument and the next – even if you limit yourself to that area.

Singing

The difference between a piano that can sing and one that can't is quite easy to hear. A listening tip: if you play a chord or two notes at once on a good instrument and keep the keys pressed down, you'll often notice that the sound seems to start singing just after you play the keys – as though the notes are reinforcing each other. You can hear this effect more clearly in the bass than in the higher octaves.

The attack

So it's important to listen to what happens after the hammer has struck the strings and, especially, to what happens at the very moment it strikes. Much of the difference in tone between one instrument and another lies there, in the *attack*. The attack can be very bright, or be soft, warm, felty, firm, indistinct or solid, just to give a few examples.

Bright or warm

Pianists often divide pianos into two broad groups: bright sounding and warm sounding. Asian-built pianos are usually placed in the first category, European instruments in the second and American ones somewhere in between. There may be as many exceptions to this rule as there are pianos, however. Or pianists, for that matter.

Taste

When two people listen to the same piano, they'll often use very different words to describe what they hear. What one considers shrill and thin (and so not attractive), another will think bright, sparkling and refined (and so not unattractive). Equally, what one describes as romantic and velvety, the other will call dull and woolly. It's all about taste – and the words you use to describe your own.

Style

What you like often coincides with the style you play. Jazz musicians often choose a brighter sounding instrument, for example. A thundering, heavily orchestrated piece may sound better on one piano and something airy and fast better on another; and a large choir and a salsa band will require different piano sounds. In other words, there's no such thing as the 'best' piano.

7. SILENT, PLAYER AND DIGITAL PIANOS

More and more upright pianos feature a muting system and a built-in sound module so that you can play without disturbing your neighbours. But there's much more you can buy than that. This chapter is about the ways in which you can play the piano silently, about pianos that play by themselves, and about digital pianos.

On an upright with a muting system a rubber-lined strip stops the hammers just before they hit the strings, so that no one can hear you play. Only the sound of the keys and the action remains audible. When using the muting system, you wear a pair of headphones to listen to the sounds of a digital piano: these are produced by the sound module, which is usually fitted under the keyboard, either to the right or the left.

Just like an acoustic

This digital piano behaves just like the acoustic piano it's been added to. It sounds louder when you play with more force – and the other way around – and if you press down the right-hand pedal, everything sustains, just like an ordinary piano.

Optical sensors

The movements of the keys are picked up by sensors. Usually they are optical sensors, one under each key, which respond to little beams of light; this type of sensor doesn't affect the feel of the piano. However, the keyboard does feel slightly different when the muting system is on; this is mainly because the hammers don't move quite as far.

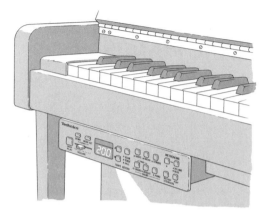

A sound module with extensive options (Technics)

Simple
The simplest sound modules have only a volume control and one or two headphone outputs. Having two headphone outputs is handy for lessons or playing duets.

More sounds
Slightly more elaborate models usually offer a greater variety of sounds. Besides samples (digital recordings) of one or more grand pianos or uprights, they may have samples of electric pianos, a few organs, a harpsichord or a string section. There are even modules that offer you a choice of hundreds of different instruments.

Piano sounds
A tip: in the end, most pianists use mainly the piano sounds, and don't really use the rest. So pay special attention to the quality of those sounds, just as if you were listening to an acoustic piano. There can be quite considerable differences between different makes.

Metronome and reverb
There may be a metronome built into the piano, and on some types you can set the volume as well as the tempo. With built-in *reverb* you can make the piano sound a little less dry in the headphones. If you have more sounds, you'll usually have more of these types of effects to choose from too; for instance a *chorus*, which is often used to make the sound of a digital 'electric' piano slightly fuller.

Recording

A built-in digital *sequencer* or *recorder* records what you play. So, for example, you can record the right-hand part of a piece and then play the left-hand part along to it. Or you can play back what you have just recorded simply to hear what you sounded like. Or you can record an idea for your own piece, or play a duet without needing to find another pianist to play with. Again, you listen through headphones, and often there are special outputs too (*line out* or *audio out*) to connect the module to an amplifier.

Audio in

If there is an input for sound signals (marked *line in* or *audio in*) you can play along with special CDs on which the piano part has been omitted, without disturbing anyone.

Operation

With some makes you operate the sound module by pressing buttons on the box itself; others have a number of controls to the left of the keyboard or somewhere else close to hand. While these may be easier to reach, they are also more visible.

Polyphony

Brochures will often say something about the number of notes that the sound module can produce at the same time. If the module offers *16-voice polyphony,* it can produce sixteen notes at once. That may sound like a lot – after all, you only have ten fingers – but in fact you'll often need more. After all, if you sustain a chord and carry on playing other notes you soon use more than ten sounds or voices simultaneously. 64-voice polyphony should always give you enough capacity, whatever you play.

MIDI

Many sound modules also have MIDI connections, which allow you to connect your piano to a synthesizer, or to a computer. What good is that?

Piano keys, synthesizer sounds

If you link a synthesizer to the MIDI output of your sound module, you can trigger the synth sounds by playing the keys of your piano. You can do it the other way around, too: you can operate the sound module from a keyboard or a computer connected to the MIDI input. In other words: MIDI is a system you can use to connect electronic musical instruments, computers and other electronic equipment to each other.

In and out

MIDI stands for *Musical Instrument Digital Interface*: a digital connector for musical instruments. The simplest sound modules only have a MIDI output: this allows you to control other instruments from your piano. More complex models also have a MIDI in, and sometimes other options.

Computer

If you connect a computer to your piano and you have the right software, you can use MIDI to print out what you play in musical notation, or to record it digitally and adapt it later.

Names

Pianos with a muting system and built-in digital piano are sometimes called *hybrid pianos*: they are both acoustic and digital. Well-known names for this type of system include Anytime, City Piano, DuoVox, Night & Day, Silent piano, StillAcoustic, QuietTime and VARIO System.

Prices

Most of these systems cost somewhere between £1000 and £1700/$1500 and $2000 when installed in a new instrument. It always costs more to have them built into the piano you already have, partly because the instrument will need to be re-regulated. You can expect to pay from around £1900/$2500 upwards.

More information

You can read more about what you can do with sound modules, sequencers and MIDI in *The Rough Guide to Keyboards and Digital Piano.*

PLAYER PIANOS

Modern player pianos have largely the same electronics on board as pianos with muting systems. The main difference is that there is an extra jack under the far end of every key, the end connected to the action. These jacks (*solenoids*) are controlled by the sound module, and they replace the pianist's fingers.

Recording
The idea is very simple. A good pianist plays a piece on a piano with in-built sensors that register all the key and pedal movements very precisely. Everything that is played can be recorded digitally on a floppy disk, a hard disk, a CD or another storage medium.

Reproduction
Afterwards, the process is reversed. The CD or hard disk tells the jacks exactly which keys they are to push upwards and how hard, and the same goes for the pedals. The result is a modern player piano, a piano that plays itself. They don't come cheap. These systems will easily cost you £3500–5000/$5000–7500.

Famous pianists
You can use a system like that to record and reproduce your own playing, but you can also bring famous pianists into your living room – and on a real instrument they'll always sound better than on even the best hi-fi system. Or you can let a master pianist play the right-hand part, while you play the left-hand part yourself. Some systems work with floppy disks, others with CDs or even videodiscs. Most new computer techniques and storage systems quickly find their way into this type of system.

Brands
Brands include ConcertMaster (Baldwin), Disklavier (Yamaha), PianoDisc and QRS/Pianomation.

DIGITAL PIANOS
Instead of having a muting system and a sound module retro-fitted, you can buy a complete digital piano to go with your acoustic piano – if you have room for it. You can read all about it in *The Rough Guide to Keyboard and Digital Piano*: only the most important points are listed on the next pages.

A good keyboard

You can buy a good digital piano for around £1000/ $1500, sometimes even less. More than anything else, what makes a good digital piano is a keyboard that feels as though you are playing an 'ordinary' piano. For this reason, these keyboards often have small hammers whose only function is to mimic the feel of a piano action. They come with names such as *hammer action, hammered action* and *weighted action*. Some digital grands have a real grand piano action, the only difference being that there are no strings.

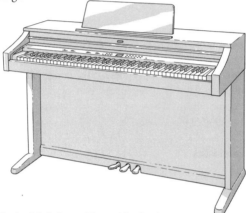

A simple digital piano with a weighted action

Touch-sensitive

Practically every digital piano is *touch-sensitive*: if you play the keys harder, the sound is louder. And they should not just sound louder but also a little brighter – just like an acoustic piano.

Not quite the same sound

However good a digital piano is, it will never sound the same as an acoustic piano. The most important reason is that the sound comes from a set of speakers, rather than being produced by a soundboard.

No strings

Digital pianos also sound different because they don't have strings, and non-existent strings can't resonate or 'sing' along, for instance when you press the right-hand pedal. This makes the sound of the instrument noticeably less rich and present. That said, there are models in which even that effect is simulated.

Learning to play

Even then, you will still to learn to play better on a good acoustic piano than on a digital – and the difference between acoustic and digital instruments gets more noticeable the better you develop your technique.

Options

Most digital pianos have more options than the sound modules usually installed in acoustic pianos: more sounds, more effects, a more versatile sequencer (with more tracks, a larger memory and more sophisticated editing facilities), and so on. MIDI and other connections are virtually always present.

The price

Digital pianos cost less than acoustic ones. For £2000–£4000/$2500–5,000 you can get yourself the very best, with hundreds of sounds and all the options you could wish for. These instruments don't last as long as acoustic pianos and they lose their value a lot sooner. However, they need no maintenance and don't have to be tuned, voiced or regulated.

8. ACCESSORIES

Playing the piano is more enjoyable if you are sitting on a good piano stool (bench in the USA), not on an ordinary chair. What other accessories are there? A lamp to help you read the music and to see what you're doing, a set of castor cups to avoid damage to the floor, and, if you really need to sound louder, a set of transducers.

Most pianists sit on a rectangular stool or bench. When you're sitting on a broad seat like this, it's easier to bend to the left or right if you need to. Playing is easier and less tiring if you are sitting at the right height. For this reason, the height of most piano stools can be adjusted.

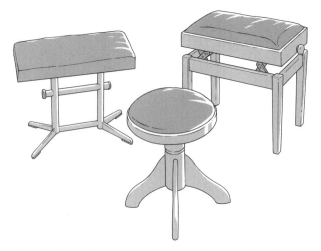

A stool with a spring system, a swivel-top stool and an adjustable stool

Springs or pneumatic

Other benches work just like an office chair, with a built-in spring or pneumatic suspension. That's especially handy if the height has to be readjusted frequently. Stools with a storage space under the seat are not usually adjustable, but they are available in various heights.

Legs

You can sometimes choose between straight, round, twisted or other shaped legs, or between different colours so that the bench will perfectly suit your piano and the look of your room.

Swivel-top

Swivel-top stools are piano stools with a round seat – you adjust the height by turning the seat around. Some are designed so that the seat won't move up or down every time you stand up or sit down. Expect to pay around £80/$125 for a good swivel-top that still won't wobble years later.

Lining

Only the expensive benches and stools are covered with real leather. Synthetic leather is tougher and easier to keep clean than real leather or textile. On the other hand, textile is less sticky than synthetic leather can be. Black is the most popular colour, but not the only one.

More expensive

A good piano stool will cost at least £120/$200. More money will buy extra sturdiness and a longer lifespan, and often a more exclusive design. Some people take exclusivity to extremes: particular stools can sell for as much as £500/$800, and antiques might cost £2000/$2500 or more. Other specialities include *duet benches* on which you can adjust the height of each seat separately, or stools with a seat that tips forwards slightly.

LAMPS

By far the majority of dedicated piano lamps are made of brass and have a fairly classical design, but there are others with a more modern look. Both types come with either halogen lamps or ordinary bulbs. There are special versions for grand pianos that can be clamped to the music stand. If the lamp needs to stand on the back part of an upright's lid, because the front part is open for playing, then a model with a 'boom' can be handy. A good piano lamp costs about £40/$60 or more. Ordinary lamps often have the drawback that the light isn't distributed across the keyboard sufficiently well: a piano lamp usually has two bulbs.

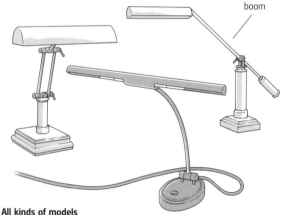

boom

All kinds of models

CASTOR CUPS

Castors, small ones especially, tend to leave deep marks in most types of carpet. The solution is to get a set of castor cups. Of course, the castors have to be lifted out of the cups if you want to move the piano.

All kinds of materials

Castor cups are available in all kinds of materials, from wood (matching the colour of the piano or the floor) to glass and plastic, and with prices from a few pounds or dollars to over forty or fifty.

Keeping the noise down

A piano on castor cups transmits slightly less sound to the floor. There are even special castor cups designed to have a dampening effect.

Too low

If the keyboard of a piano is very low – or if you are very tall – the whole instrument can be placed onto extra high castor cups. But be aware that the higher the castor cups are, the harder it is to reach the pedals comfortably.

Various materials and heights

TRANSDUCERS

If you often have to play amplified, in a band, for instance, you'll soon realize that most microphones aren't up to the job. Transducers usually work much better.

Vibration-sensitive

Transducers or *piezo pickups* are thin strips or discs made of a vibration-sensitive material, which 'pick up' the vibrations of the instrument and send them to the amplifier. Similar pickups are used on acoustic guitars, violins and other instruments. On a piano it's best to stick one or two to the back or the underside of the soundboard, between the ribs. Usually, one transducer is not enough to pick up all the sound of such a large instrument.

Where to put them

The best place to attach the pickups for optimum results varies with the instrument and the type of pickup. You'll often find good tips in the manual that comes with the pickups.

Price

Two piano transducers will cost £120−160/$150−200 or more. Specialized microphones capable of capturing the sound of a piano properly cost much more, and even then they are better suited for use in the studio than on stage.

9. MAINTENANCE

A piano needs less maintenance than most other instruments. All you really need to do is to keep it clean and make sure that the humidity and temperature in your home don't cause problems.

You are better off leaving such tasks as moving a piano, tuning it, or major maintenance to professionals. Chapter 10 tells you all about that. But there are a few things you can do on your own.

Polyester lacquer

Instruments finished with polyester lacquer are easy to keep clean by very lightly rubbing them with a soft, lint-free cloth. Clean in long, straight lines rather than in circles and exert as little pressure as possible: strange though it may sound, dust can scratch. A very slightly damp cloth picks up dust more easily. Dusters will do the job, but so will an old plain T-shirt. A dishcloth may be too coarse. You can remove most 'fresh' fingerprints by first breathing on them, so that the lacquer mists over.

Satin-finish

Fingerprints, dust and even very fine scratches are much less visible on a satin-finish or open-pore instrument than on an ebonized (high-gloss black) piano.

French polished or waxed

On French-polished pianos or instruments treated with wax, a soft, dry cloth will usually do, provided the instrument is cleaned regularly.

Cleaners

Special cleaners are available for every type of finish, costing £6–10/$10–15 a bottle. That doesn't sound cheap, but you may only use a cleaner once a year, so it'll last a long time. The packaging or instructions always tell you which types of lacquer or material the cleaner is suitable for.

Soap

To remove marks on high-gloss and satin lacquer finishes you can add a little soft soap (mild washing-up liquid or shampoo) to the water you are using to moisten the cloth.

Polishing polyester

A polyester finish quickly shows up very fine scratches. To combat this, there are cleaners available that also polish the surface very slightly. Do always dust off the instrument first. Some cleaners have an anti-static (dust repellent) effect. Deeper scratches or dents can be filled; there are special 'sticks' available for the job, but if you want an invisible repair it's best to get a craftsman to do it.

French polish

A French-polished finish can also be treated by very lightly buffing it; ask a piano dealer for the right cleaner. Any damage should be repaired by a professional. Getting a whole instrument French polished costs thousands.

Wax

If you have a piano finished with wax, or a satin-finish instrument whose lacquer has worn thin, you can treat it very lightly with beeswax once a year. Experts usually advise against using a wax that contains silicones. Never use wax on synthetic wood (artificial 'veneer' or photoprint).

Keys

Clean the keys with a slightly damp cloth. If that doesn't help, and the keys are plastic-covered, spray a very small amount of glass cleaner onto the cloth – not onto the keys themselves – or use a special key cleaner. Now and again, clean the sides of the keys too: the sides get dirty when you play the neighbouring keys. The colour of ebonized black keys can sometimes rub off: if that is the case, don't use the same cloth to clean the white keys.

The sides of the keys get dirty too

Ivory

Don't use glass cleaner or other cleaners on ivory-covered keys, and dry them off at once: ivory is sensitive to moisture. Another tip: only use a cloth if you are absolutely certain its colour won't run.

Dust

A vacuum cleaner will help you get most of the dust out of an upright piano. That means first taking off the lower panel, which is usually only attached with a simple clamp. Don't touch the wood, the strings or other parts with the vacuum cleaner tube, and always use a soft brush attachment. The easiest way to get dust out of awkward corners is to use a clean paintbrush. Keep the vacuum cleaner nearby to get rid of the dust.

Grand piano

You can clean the inside of a grand piano in much the same way, although dust under the frame is harder to get rid of. A feather duster may help, if you use it carefully. You can also try to blow the dust from under the frame. Of course, most of the dust will drift back down and settle in or next to the instrument. Two tips: only use a hair dryer if it blows cold or lukewarm air; some vacuum cleaners also have a 'blow' setting.

The action

Dust and dirt get onto the dampers of a grand piano too.

You can carefully remove it with a dry cloth, or – very carefully – by using a vacuum cleaner with a very soft brush fitting. You should leave any other cleaning of the action to your tuner or your technician.

Moths

The anti-moth treatment the felt receives in the factory eventually wears off. Keeping it free from dust helps to keep moths away. If moths are already a problem or you think they might be, hang a piece of odour-free moth paper on the inside of the upper frame.

Woodworm

Playing your instrument helps prevent woodworm because they don't like vibrating wood. If a lot of holes and tunnels are visible in the wood, call an expert.

Questions

When you buy an instrument in a shop, you will often be told what maintenance is required. You can also try asking your tuner if you have any questions. There is space to note them down at the back of this book.

PREVENTION

You can avoid a lot of cleaning, polishing and repairs by following the tips below.

Keep the lid closed

Close the instrument when you are not playing it. Otherwise, dust will settle in the mechanism and the windings of the bass strings. Wood-coloured instruments may begin to discolour unevenly if the fall is always open: the wood will keep its colour only where the fall rests against the upper panel.

Clean hands

Keep the keys (top and sides!) clean by washing your hands before you start playing. It really does make a difference. You can avoid covering your piano with finger-prints by handling the lids by the bottom edge or sides as much as possible.

No flowers, plants or drinks

Don't put flowers or plants on top of the instrument. The insides and the keys are very sensitive to moisture, and the outside often is too. French polish is especially vulnerable. For the same reason, don't put drinks on the cabinet or on the key blocks (the small flat areas at either end of the keyboard).

Scratches

If you do put a photo frame, a lamp or anything else on the instrument, stick a layer of felt underneath it. A tip: black polyester scratches especially easily. Even music books can scratch the surface.

Candles

Spilled candle-wax is difficult to remove without scratching, and wax between the keys is especially annoying.

Strings and felt

Don't touch the strings or felt with bare hands because your natural skin secretions and the acids they contain are not good for them: felt gets greasy and strings rust.

Cover

If you often have a lot of people visiting it might be a good idea to buy a cover. They are available for both grand pianos and uprights and they completely cover the instrument.

Moving

At some time you may want to shift your piano within your house or apartment. If you are in any doubt, leave this to the professionals, especially if you are planning to move it to another room. This will help prevent damage to your back, your house and the instrument itself. A tip: small castors don't usually roll very well.

DRY AND MOIST, HOT AND COLD

In many houses, the humidity and temperature are so steady that a piano can happily grow old there. But if the air is too dry or too humid, if the humidity changes fast and often, or if the temperature in the room is very low for a time, you can get all kinds of problems. The soundboard can crack, panels can warp, keys can stick and tuning-pins come loose. Fortunately, all of those things are preventable.

Dry

If it's freezing outside and the central heating is on indoors, the air gets drier and drier. Convection heaters and air conditioning also make the air extra dry. Lips get chapped, and wood contracts. If the soundboard contracts, the crown (page 60) gets lower, reducing the tension on the strings so that they go out of tune.

Moist

In summer, the air is at it's most moist. In humid conditions, wood expands. That means the tension on the soundboard increases, and with it the tension on the strings. If it gets really humid, keys can stick, just like doors and windows.

All kinds of other parts can suffer from moisture: damp hammer heads produce a 'squidgy' sound, the action gets noticeably heavier and strings can rust. Old houses with gas fires are usually quite damp.

Forty to sixty percent humidity

Many experts say the best humidity level for pianos (and for people) is between 40% and 60%, although other figures are sometimes quoted. It needn't matter if the humidity briefly goes outside of that range, but if it lasts for days you may have problems.

Changes

It's at least as important that the humidity doesn't change too fast. You should take that into account if you move an instrument from an old house with a gas fire to a much drier apartment with central heating and air conditioning – or the other way around.

Hygrometer

You can measure humidity using a *hygrometer*, available from all piano shops and many opticians. The cheapest models, which are fairly inexpensive, have a dial and a pointer. Digital hygrometers cost more, but are more accurate and often include a thermometer.

Calibrating

There is another difference. A dial-type hygrometer, which uses a hair to measure the humidity level, gets sluggish and becomes steadily less responsive. However, if you leave it outside for a night the moist air will refresh it for a whole year. Or better still, you can recalibrate it yourself. Around the time of year when the weather gets colder and you switch the heating back on, wrap it in a wet cloth for a quarter of an hour and immediately afterwards set the pointer to 98%.

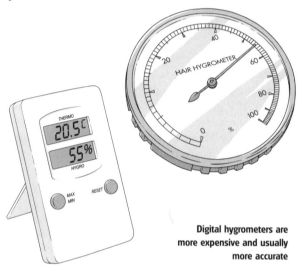

Digital hygrometers are more expensive and usually more accurate

Sunlight and heating

Wood heats up and dries out if you leave it too close to a heater, and putting a piano above a heating vent is asking for trouble. Direct sunlight is just as bad, certainly if it shines straight onto the soundboard of the instrument. Lacquer is easily damaged by direct sunlight too.

Temperature

Pianos are like people when it comes to temperature. Around 20°C (65–70°F) is ideal, but a few degrees more or less is fine too. However, if it gets much colder than 16°C you may have problems, so if you go on holiday during the winter, leave the heating on a very low setting. The more steady the temperature and humidity, the more stable the tuning of the instrument will be.

Extra measures

Whether you need to take extra measures to keep the humidity at the right level depends on a lot of things. For instance, houseplants and an open kitchen cause extra moisture in the air, whereas a very well-stocked bookcase helps to keep the humidity a little more constant. A piano is better off standing near an inner wall than a thin outer wall and if you put it in a cellar, you'll probably be faced with damp. These are just a few of the factors you may have to consider: only a hygrometer can tell you precisely what you need to know.

Too dry?

Really, the biggest problem is excessively dry air, and the worst times are when it's freezing outside. There are all kinds of steps you can take to avoid dry air. Special water containers hung on the radiators help a little, but not usually enough. If the humidity falls suddenly, a stopgap solution is to hang some damp towels over the radiators. This is effective, but not very stylish. As a last resort you can also stick a rolled-up newspaper into a container half-full of water and stand it in the bottom of the piano. The newspaper helps the water to evaporate, but it's still not a very fast process. What's more, it may go mouldy, the moisture may cause the strings or frame to rust, the whole thing could fall over or – more likely still – simply be forgotten.

Dampp-Chaser

The Dampp-Chaser, one of the most popular internal climate control systems, keeps the humidity level inside the instrument stable. If it's too dry, the built-in *hygrostat* automatically switches on the moisturizer; if the air is too damp, it activates the drying unit. A warning light comes on when you need to refill the tank with water, which is easy to do with a special tube. The system costs around £250/$500, including installation. In some cases your guarantee may be extended if you have a Dampp-Chaser installed when you buy an instrument.

Other systems

There are many other internal systems for sale, ranging from very simple and inexpensive water-filled tubes to more advanced humidifiers, hygrostats and heating elements. They differ in price, of course, and also in the amount of attention they require.

The whole room

There are also various types of devices to humidify the whole room. This extends the benefits of a better climate to you and to wooden cupboards and floors, for instance. Each system has its own advantages and drawbacks: some of the most frequently met with are listed below.

Hot and cold systems

Steam humidifiers are available from around £50/$75. They work fast and generate some extra heat, but some people find the warmth they produce too damp. What's more, you can hear some models bubbling away when they're switched on. Cold humidifier systems are quieter, but also more expensive. They take longer to work, they need quite a lot of maintenance (cleaning, filling, and so on), and some models require you to add special chemicals to the water. Some of these devices are also capable of drying the air during humid periods. Depending on how your house is heated, it may also be a good idea to have a central humidifier installed.

Look and compare

Visit a few different shops and ask about these and other systems, compare prices and energy consumption, ask whether you need any extras and what they cost, and consider the maximum volume of air each device can handle. Larger rooms may need two. You can buy them from shops that sell household appliances as well as from piano shops.

10. TRANSPORT, TUNING AND REGULATING

Most pianos need to be tuned two or more times a year if they are to sound their best. If you want to get as much enjoyment as possible from your instrument for as long as possible, it will also need regulating every few years. And of course, new strings, new hammers and many other new parts can be fitted in due course if required. All of those jobs are best left to the professionals, as is transportation.

If you need to have a piano transported, it's best to use an established firm of piano movers. If you are buying a new instrument, carriage to your home is often included in the price; if you are buying secondhand or renting it usually isn't. Ask in advance who is paying for what; for example, sometimes the cost of moving a rental piano will be deducted from the price if you later decide to buy the instrument.

Costs

The cost varies between roughly £60 and £200/$125 and $400 plus a charge for the number of miles travelled. You'll pay less if your piano is being moved to the ground floor than if it has to be hoisted to an upper floor. These days, it's quite rare for pianos to be carried up stairs; many professionals always employ hoisting equipment. In exceptional cases the price can go even higher, for example if a crane has to be used. Ask for a binding quote in advance. Of course, the firm will only give one when they know exactly what the job involves.

Indoors

Even if a piano only has to be moved from one room to another, it's a good idea to get the professionals in to do the job. Plenty of people have got themselves jammed between a piano and the banisters or doorposts before now.

Specialist movers

You can find specialist piano movers in the *Yellow Pages* or through a piano shop. The firm should be insured for any damage it may cause.

Space

Check beforehand whether the instrument will fit where you want to take it: is the door wide enough, is there enough room to turn it, can the window open wide enough and is there enough space on the stairs? Some movers will come and take a look themselves, if necessary.

Damage

If the instrument being moved is secondhand, always take a look at it together with one of the piano movers and note down any scratches and other damage. Then you'll know for certain if any damage was caused during transportation.

TUNING

A guitar or a violin has to be tuned every time it is played. Fortunately, a piano doesn't. Two or three times a year is often enough.

Out of tune

Every piano goes out of tune eventually, even if it hasn't been played, one reason being that the tension of the strings varies with changes in humidity and temperature (see page 94 and onwards). The more stable those two factors are, the more stable the tuning of the instrument will be.

Piano tuners and technicians

Tuning a piano is a job for a professional, from the 'setting' of the tuning-pins to the precise tuning of over two hundred strings. Many piano tuners are also piano technicians, which means they carry out repairs and adjustments too. Do note that anyone can set themselves up as a piano tuner or technician. However, there are professional associations that give certificates to tuners and technicians who pass a special test. Of course, not everyone wants to be a member of an association like that, which means there are also good piano tuners and technicians who don't have these certificates. A tip: ask other piano owners whether they know a good tuner, or let a piano salesperson advise you.

A job for an expert

How much

A normal tuning takes about an hour, and the price will usually be somewhere between £30 and £50/$50 and $70. Many firms and tuners offer subscriptions. This works out a little cheaper, and it also means you will automatically be reminded when it's time to have your piano tuned again.

How often

If you play about five to ten hours a week, it's usually enough to have your instrument tuned two to three times a year. If an instrument needs to be tuned more often or if it goes out of tune very quickly then something is wrong with it, or with the conditions in the room where it's standing. Either that or the tuner is not doing their job properly: a good tuner always sees that the tuning is stable.

More often

New and recently restrung instruments need to be tuned more often, one reason being that new strings will stretch before they stabilize. Some tuners say that one extra tuning per year for the first few years is enough, others prefer to give a piano two extra tunings in the first year. The particular instrument plays a role in the decision too.

Too late

If you can hear that a piano is clearly out of tune, you're really too late in getting it tuned. The more a tuner has to adjust it, the harder it is to produce a stable tuning. What's more, constant turning of the tuning-pins causes more wear to the pinblock.

Too low

Some pianos never seem to go out of tune. Should you still have them tuned regularly? Yes, because otherwise the tuning of the whole instrument will get lower and lower. If the tuning is too low, it may be difficult to play together with other musicians. What's more, the tone will suffer and it can be difficult to get the tuning back to the right pitch (see page 68).

Just moved

If a piano has just been moved, it will need to get used to its new surroundings for about two or three weeks – and there's a fair chance that it will suddenly go out of tune or not play as well during that period. If you need to have it tuned and regulated, wait until those few weeks have passed. When you buy a new instrument, this service is often included in the price.

About an hour

Tuners usually take about an hour to do the job. Even if they use an electronic tuner, they'll do most of the work by ear – which is only possible if it's quiet enough.

Electronic tuner?

There are indeed electronic tuners for pianos – and there are books which tell you how to use them. A tip: these tuners cost over £200/$1000 and they are still no more than an aid for experienced tuners. Another tip: the knowledge and experience a tuner gains during a three-year training programme is more than can be contained in a single book.

EQUAL TEMPERAMENT

A piano is difficult to tune because it has so many strings, but that's not the only reason. The fact that two tuners will always tune an instrument slightly differently gives you a clue. Below is a brief explanation of equal temperament. If you're not interested in a little musical mathematics, turn to page 105.

Twice as fast

The A that most instruments are tuned to is slightly to the right of the centre of a piano keyboard: the note a1. At that pitch, the strings vibrate at a speed of 440 vibrations per second (440 hertz). At a2 (eight white keys or an octave higher), the strings vibrate twice as fast (880 hertz).

One and a half

Similary, there are specific ratios for the other intervals. For example, if you go up a fifth (five white keys), the strings vibrate one and a half times as fast at the higher pitch.

Problem

Now, there is a slight problem, one that experts have wrestled with for centuries. In the illustration on the following page you'll see what it is: the different ratios don't match. The calculation shown above the keyboard fixes the note a2 at a different pitch from the one shown below the keyboard.

Hiding

What's the solution? The tuner 'hides' these discrepancies by tuning most of the notes a tiny bit too high or too low. The differences are so small that you can't hear them, or only just. For instance, c1 is tuned to around 260 hertz, rather than 264.

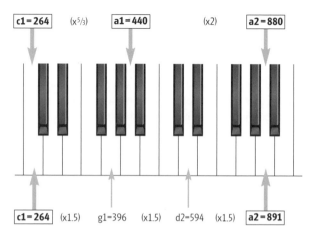

The sums don't add up

The solution

Tuners always have to decide how much they allow certain notes to deviate, and they do so by listening to the beats.

Beats

If you play c1 and g2 together on a properly tuned piano, you'll hear very soft, quite slow 'waves' in the sound, which are called beats. If you then play c1 and a1, you'll hear faster beats. They betray the fact that even a well-tuned piano is slightly 'out of tune': if a piano were perfectly tuned, you wouldn't hear them.

Even temperament

Nearly every combination of two notes will produce beats, however slightly. In other words: the discrepancies (the 'mathematical errors') are spread across the whole keyboard. The official name for this kind of tuning is equal temperament.

Differently in tune

The tuner knows how low or high each note needs to be tuned by listening very closely to those beats. Exactly which frequencies they choose to achieve a balanced tuning depends on the individual tuner. That means that a different tuner may make your piano sound just slightly different. Not out of tune, just 'differently in tune'. You may prefer one tuning to another.

In or out of tune

Finally: it is possible to tune a piano perfectly and without beats, but not without limitations or without creating other problems. For instance, if you tune a piano so that the scale of C sounds perfectly in tune, the scale of B will suddenly sound terribly out of tune. And so will the scale of A. So you'll be able to play a piece that uses the scale of C (with no sharps or flats), but a piece with four flats (in A flat major or F minor) will sound awful.

REGULATING AND VOICING

Whether an instrument needs extra attention every two years or only once a decade depends on a number of things. The more you play and the older the instrument is, the more often major maintenance will be required. On the other hand, your piano will need less frequent maintenance if you keep the fall closed when you are not playing it, if the tuner does some minor maintenance and checks the regulation and voicing as well as the tuning, if you only play for a few hours a week, and if you keep the inside of the instrument clean. The quality and the condition of the instrument also play a role. A good tuner will help you keep an eye on all of those things. If something goes wrong in the meantime, from breaking strings to sticking keys or creaking pedals, call an expert at once.

Voicing

Over the years, the felt of the hammer heads gets gradually denser and harder, which in time results in an ever-thinner, shriller tone. That's why every instrument needs to be re-voiced sooner or later (see also page 51). Hammers can be reshaped if they have become flattened by playing or the strings have worn deep grooves into them – provided there is still enough felt left and it is in good condition.

Felt, leather, wood, metal

The parts of the action wear out too, whether they are the small metal pins, the felt 'bushings' inside which the pins pivot, or the piece of leather at the hammer butt, where the jack hits it. What's more, the regulation changes with time. Not just through wear, but also because wood constantly expands and contracts. It happens so slowly that you'll barely notice it – but even so, there may come a moment when the instrument feels noticeably stiffer to play, or less responsive, or less even, or just plain awkward.

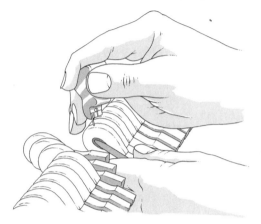

Making hammer heads softer by pricking them

A whole day

All of these things will be checked during a major service. What exactly needs doing will depend on the age and the condition of your piano, among other things. The service may be a day's work, but if the instrument is worth it you might decide to have, say, all the strings, hammers, dampers and tuning-pins replaced. An operation like that will easily cost £3500/$5000, but afterwards the instrument will sound as though it were new.

11. BACK IN TIME

The action invented by Bartolomeo Cristofori some three hundred years ago bears a striking resemblance to the one you'll find in a grand piano today. Even so, there have been plenty of developments since his day – and of course, much went before.

As early as the fourteenth century, and perhaps even earlier, there was an instrument with keys and strings: the *clavichord* (*clavis* means key, *chord* means string). When you pressed the keys down, a small brass wedge made contact with the strings. The sound was very soft, however forcefully the instrument was played.

Plucking

The *harpsichord*, which was most popular in the seventeenth and eighteenth century, sounded a lot bigger and fuller than the clavichord. Harpsichord strings are plucked by the quills of raven feathers attached to the ends of the keys.

Spinet

A *spinet* works like a harpsichord, but it is a size smaller and the strings run at a pronounced angle backwards from the keys. On the *virginal*, another variant, the strings usually run perpendicular to the keys, from left to right.

Touch-sensitive

Harpsichords, spinets and virginals are not touch-sensitive: every note sounds equally loud. This was the problem the Italian harpsichord maker Bartolomeo Cristofori

(1655–1731) set out to tackle. In or around 1698 he began building an instrument based on the harpsichord that used hammers instead of raven quills, and which would be able to play both loudly and softly.

Piano e forte

The result, which he unveiled a few years later, he christened the gravicembalo col piano e forte (harpsichord with soft and loud). A good quarter of a century after his first experiments Cristofori came up with an improved action, which was very similar to the present-day system.

Pianoforte, fortepiano

The full name of the instrument was soon shortened to *pianoforte* or *fortepiano*. Just like harpsichords and spinets, these forerunners of the modern piano are still used to play old music. The main difference is that the tone of a pianoforte or *hammerklavier* is a bit thinner, glassier and shorter than that of a modern grand piano.

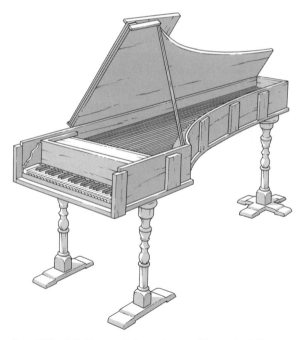

One of Cristofori's first grand pianos. A range of four-and-a-half octaves, no pedals, leather hammer heads and two-string unisons for each note.

Square piano

From about 1750 to 1850, the *square piano* was very popular. Its horizontal strings ran from left to right within a rectangular cabinet.

A square piano with over five octaves and a lyre with three pedals
(Pleyel, 1816)

Vertical

The first instruments in which the strings were fitted vertically were built midway through the eighteenth century. Names like *giraffe piano* and *pyramid piano* indicate that such instruments came in all kinds of shapes and sizes. The precursor of the modern upright piano appeared around 1800. Matthias Müller, Isaac Hawkins and Robert Wornum are the three names most often mentioned as important in its development.

Improved

Since Cristofori's time a number of things have been changed, invented and improved. For instance, in 1822 the Frenchman Sebastian Érard devised *the double escape mechanism* or *repetition mechanism,* the system that allows you to play rapid repeated notes on a grand piano. Before that, he had already introduced agraffes and other innovations. His compatriot Henri Pape was also responsible for countless inventions, from felt hammer heads to the cross-strung upright piano. Steinway, a manufacturer that acquired more than a hundred patents, produced the first cross-strung grands in the middle of the nineteenth century.

Louder

In order to give pianists more volume and a bigger sound strings continued to increase their thickness over the years. In turn, those strings needed bigger hammer heads to set them in motion, and the increased string tension required a cast-iron frame, which the American piano maker Alpheus Babcock patented in 1825. The soundboard also became steadily thicker, and the number of octaves grew from four and a half to more than seven.

Player piano

A very different invention, dating back to the end of the nineteenth century, is the player piano: a piano which works much like a barrel organ, with paper rolls punched with

An English piano built around 1800 (Robert Knight, London; Cristofori collection, Amsterdam)

holes which tell the mechanism when to play each note. These days, player pianos use digital technology (see chapter 7).

A hundred years

Little has changed in the last hundred years or so, but of course piano makers have not been idle. The results of their efforts range from synthetic components to player grands with built-in CD players, and from springs and magnets to help uprights repeat faster to special cabinet designs.

Only a few

There have also been a lot of innovations that never really caught on. Glass grands, for example, or instruments with eight extra keys per octave that permit the playing of microtones, double grands with two keyboards and two soundboards, or even instruments for left-handed pianists, with the bass notes on the right.

Special cabinet design (Van Urk)

12. THE FAMILY

Not all of the instruments in this chapter are direct relatives of the piano but they all belong to the wider family of keyboard instruments. Here's a brief introduction to the members of that family, both old and new.

Pianos belong to the family of string instruments, like guitars and violins. Within that family they are part of the group of keyboard instruments, as do the harpsichord, the spinet and the fortepiano mentioned in the previous chapter. In this chapter you'll find descriptions of the most important keyboard instruments. The digital piano, which appeared in the early 1980s, was discussed in chapter 7.

With hammers

The only relative without keys included in this chapter is the *dulcimer*. Just like a piano, the strings of this instrument are sounded by striking them with hammers. The difference is that you hold the hammers yourself. The most highly developed form of the dulcimer is the *cimbalom* or *tsambal*, found in Hungarian and Romanian gypsy orchestras.

With metal bars

A *celesta* looks like a small piano but is actually a glockenspiel with keys: the hammers strike metal bars, which produce a ringing tone. The sound is very soft, and the instrument is rarely used outside the classical orchestra.

With reeds

Many *accordions* have an 'ordinary' keyboard for the right hand while the bass notes are played by the left hand on a bank of black buttons. When you stretch or squeeze the bellows, air flows past metal reeds, making them vibrate, on the same principle as the mouth organ.

With forks
The *electric piano* is the forerunner of the digital piano. Instead of strings, most electric pianos have metal forks, reeds or rods which are struck by hammers. The vibrations are picked up by one or more magnetic pickups (like those of an electric guitar) and then sent to the amplifier. Electric pianos are no longer being built, but plenty are still in use.

With pipes
An organ may vaguely resemble a piano, but it is actually a very different instrument, and one that requires a very different technique. One major difference is that whereas a piano note decays after a while, if you press an organ key the note goes on until you release the key. On classical or church organs, air is blown through a large number of pipes. Naturally, that produces a very different sound to a set of piano strings. Another difference is that an organ is not touch-sensitive. On the other hand, most organs do have a volume pedal and a tremendous range of different timbres.

With electronics
You'll always find a volume pedal on an electronic organ, which may also have a *pedal board*, an oversized keyboard operated by the feet. (Church organs almost invariably have such a pedal board.) Digital versions of all kinds of organs have also appeared in recent years.

With tonewheels
As is the case with electric pianos, there are electronic organs which are no longer in production but are still widely used. The best-known example is the Hammond organ. This so-called *tonewheel organ* was later succeeded by a digital model.

With samples
Keyboards or *home keyboards* are really part of the organ family. Apart from organ sounds they have dozens,

sometimes hundreds, of other sounds, ranging from guitars and strings to complete drum sets, clarinets, rain showers and helicopters. All of those sounds have been sampled (see page 80). Keyboards also come with a standard automatic accompaniment feature: play a chord, choose a tempo and you hear a complete accompanying orchestra – so all you have to do is play the melody or a solo.

A keyboard: hundreds of sounds, automatic accompaniment, a recorder, built-in amplification,and much more (Gem)

Piano?

Most keyboards also give you the choice of several piano sounds. Even so, you can't 'play the piano' properly on this instrument, because most keyboards don't have a weighted action (see page 84).

Synthesizer

To *synthesize* means to produce a new object by combining various simpler parts. With a synthesizer you can make your own sounds. The instrument usually has a number of basic sounds which you can process, combine and change in all kinds of ways until you get the sound you're looking for.

More and more alike

The differences between instruments like synthesizers, keyboards and digital pianos are getting ever smaller: you can buy digital pianos with automatic accompaniments, keyboards with synthesizer options, synthesizers with pre-installed sounds and many more combinations. *The Rough Guide to Keyboards and Digital Piano* takes a closer look at all of those digital instruments, and also at *workstations*, *samplers* and other instruments and equipment.

13. HOW THEY'RE MADE

Some piano factories build their instruments one by one, others have production lines. Some factories produce thirty pianos per year, others three hundred, three thousand, thirty thousand or even more. There are many differences between the way the various factories work, but broadly speaking uprights and grand pianos are built in the way described below.

Building a piano takes time. A top model can easily take more than two years to craft, from the moment the first planks are sawn to the final tuning. The wood used for expensive instruments has often been dried and cured for five or even ten years.

Soundboard

Most soundboards are made of solid spruce planks about four inches (10 cm) wide. The ribs are glued at right angles to the grain of the soundboard, at the back of the instrument. The bridges and the metal bridge pins over which the strings will run are attached to the other side.

Frame

The frame is made in a special foundry. Afterwards it is filed and sanded smooth, drilled and finished. The holes for the two hundred-plus tuning-pins must be drilled in exactly the right places.

Strings

Like the frame, the steel strings are almost always purchased from an outside supplier. The only part of string manufacture which piano factories often do in house is the winding of the bass strings. This involves turning a string (the core) and winding the copper wire around it, a job which is sometimes still done by hand.

The first tuning

Once the pinblock is in place, the strings are stretched over the soundboard and tuned for the first time. Since there are no hammers yet, the tuner plucks the strings as a guitarist would. This process is called chipping. After tuning the entire structure, consisting of the frame with backposts, soundboard, strings and pinblock, is given time to settle. The strings, now under tension, are allowed to stretch until they reach a fairly stable length.

The cabinet

Meanwhile, in a different part of the factory, the cabinet is being manufactured. Curved wooden parts, like some falls or the rim of a grand piano, are usually bent into shape using large presses or clamps.

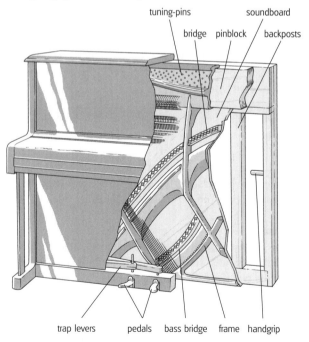

The cabinet, the backposts and other parts

Lacquers

Most high-gloss instruments are given a thick coat of polyester lacquer which is repeatedly polished to make the surface even and then buffed mirror-smooth. Instruments with a transparent high-gloss finish are first stained to give them the right colour and to bring out the figure or pattern of the wood better.

Satin-finish

On satin-finish cabinets one or more very thin layers of cellulose nitrate lacquer are applied after the staining stage to protect the wood.

Sawing the keyboard

The keyboard is sawn from a large piece of layered wood, like a kind of jigsaw puzzle. The black keys are small plastic or wooden bars which are glued on afterwards.

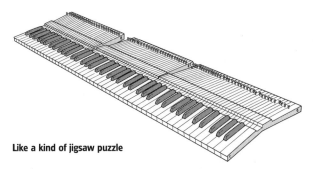

Like a kind of jigsaw puzzle

Installed

Once the frame, soundboard and strings have been installed in the cabinet, the action, the keyboard and the pedals are fitted.

Regulation

The regulation of the instrument takes a lot of time if it's to be done properly. For example, all the keys must be perfectly balanced, so weights are used to determine how much lead, if any, needs to be added to each key. In addition, each key must be exactly level with all the others, and be able to be pressed down exactly the same amount. All the dampers must respond equally quickly. And so must all the hammers, all the set-off buttons, all the pilots, all the repetition springs, all the whippen top flanges, and so on.

Voicing and tuning

Proper voicing is a time-consuming business too: the felt hammer heads are pricked by needles, one by one, to give them the correct hardness. Often instruments will be voiced more than once, just as they are tuned and regulated several times. What's more, better-quality instruments are 'played in' by machine for many hours before they leave the factory.

14. THE BRANDS

There are hundreds of piano brands, with famous names, obscure names, family names and imaginary names. This chapter tells you what you need to know, and introduces the most important brands.

All of those hundreds of brand names exist because there used to be hundreds of different factories. These were mainly small factories, producing only a few pianos each year, but each with its own brand name. Many of those firms have disappeared, to be replaced by larger factories which often build instruments under a number of brand names.

Germany

The piano is an Italian invention, and many of the early improvements came from France and England. Even so, it is the German manufacturers who have built up the most impressive reputation. As well as finished instruments, almost all of the well-known 'branded parts' used by factories all over the world come from Germany, from Kluge keyboards to Abel hammer heads. What's more, German manufacturers produce few instruments costing less than £5000/$7000 or so.

Bought or invented

With such a pedigree it's no wonder there are so many piano brands with German or German-sounding names, even though they are not built there – just as classical guitars are often given Spanish names. Some of these names are invented, but others are brand names bought from manufacturers who went out of business.

Where from?

In other words, a brand name won't always tell you much about the origin of an instrument. But nor will simply knowing which country it comes from. For instance, you can buy Chinese pianos with European parts, and European pianos with Chinese parts are just as common. There are Japanese makes which are completely assembled in Europe or America, rather like cars. And these days perfectly good instruments are made in Russia or China too, even though those countries haven't yet developed good reputations for building pianos.

More names

There are quite a number of piano factories, some of them in Europe and America, which make instruments for various brands. Some only produce pianos in one price range, others make instruments which fall into quite different categories. And sometimes, identical instruments from the same factory are sold under different brand names at very different prices – which is something to bear in mind when visiting different shops. Incidentally, this is not a trick played only with musical instruments.

The right price

Fortunately though, the majority of instruments are worth what they cost. It is still always a good idea to visit several shops to hear their views about the different brands. After all, every salesperson has their own opinion – and not just about the smaller or lesser-known brands.

House brands

Not all makes are for sale in all piano shops. For instance, some brands have only a limited number of dealers. Then there are the so-called *house brands* or *stencil brands*: piano shops, importers and distributors may order all kinds of factory pianos which are then 'badged' with their own brand names. Sometimes those instruments have certain features consciously chosen by the dealer (house brands), sometimes the name is the only thing which is really different about them (stencil brands). With most house brands, the nameplate is not cast as part of the frame as it normally would be. To help you recognize such instruments, be aware that what appears to be a cast nameplate may sometimes be a moulded synthetic one in the same colour as the frame.

The brands

There are only a limited number of brands that you'll find in a broad range of shops. The best-known are described very briefly below. Other brands are covered later in this chapter, divided by country. The information shown may easily become out-of-date: a brand currently being built in Europe may, in a few years, be imported from Asia, or the other way around. There are also countless brands you won't find here – which doesn't necessarily mean they're not good instruments. You can find more information in other specialist books and on the Internet (see Want to Know More? on page 134).

Bechstein (1853) is the best-known and oldest of the three brands owned by the German Bechstein Gruppe, which itself was taken over by Baldwin in 1963. The two others, W. Hoffmann (1904) and Zimmermann (1884), joined this group in the early Nineties. Bechstein instruments are the most expensive from this house, Hoffman the most affordable.

Bohemia is one of the great Czech names. The brands Schlögl and Rieger-Kloss belong to the same company, which has been building upright pianos and grands since 1871. Bohemia also makes, or used to make, pianos for a number of other brands, including Fibich and Hofmann & Czerny.

You'll find the name August Förster on both Czech and German pianos. In fact they are two separate brands which did originate from the same firm but which no longer have anything to do with each other. The Czech company is part of Petrof; the German Försters, which come from a much smaller factory, are in a higher price range.

GROTRIAN-STEINWEG Between 1855 and 1860, Friedrich Grotrian built pianos in partnership with Theodor Steinweg, son of the founder of Steinway. In America, the family firm Grotrian-Steinweg sells its pianos under the brand name Grotrian, in order to avoid confusion.

KAWAI
Piano-maker Koichi Kawai learned the craft while working for Yamaha. The now second-largest Japanese piano factory, set up in 1927, also builds digital pianos and supplies acoustic instruments for other makes in the lower-middle to higher-middle price range.

PETROF Petrof (1864), the Czech brand based at Europe's largest factory, produces uprights and grands in virtually all sizes. Scholze, Förster and Rösler are three separate factories which form part of the Petrof group. These companies produce instruments in a slightly lower price range. Petrof also supplies instruments and parts for numerous other brands.

PLEYEL Pleyel was founded in 1807 by the French composer Ignace Pleyel. Having been based in Germany for some time, the brand moved back to France in the 1990s. Pleyel mainly produces pianos in the higher-middle price range. The brands Gaveau, Rameau and Érard, owned by the same company, are priced slightly lower. Schulmann is a cheaper, Asian-made Pleyel brand.

SAUTER Besides 'classical' models, the German company Sauter (1819) makes various modern uprights in striking designs with matching stools. The firm has also developed its own repetition system.

SCHIMMEL Schimmel (1885) is one of the largest European manufacturers. As well as building classical models, this German firm has always been a leading innovator. For example, it produced a plexiglass grand piano as early as 1951. It also took over the Pleyel group in the early 1970s.

SEILER Like some other German makes, Seiler is still run by descendants of its founder. The firm set up by Eduard Seiler in 1849 uses a repetition system developed by the Dutch engineer H.J. Venlo, and has been one of Europe's larger manufacturers for many years.

YAMAHA The one-man organ factory started by the Japanese Torakusu Yamaha in 1889 is now the world's largest builder of musical instruments, ranging from grand and upright pianos to digital instruments, and from trumpets to drums – not to mention motorbikes, hi-fi equipment and bathtubs! The Eterna piano brand is manufactured for Yamaha in China.

YOUNG CHANG The best known Korean brand is Young Chang, one of the many Asian companies in which German experts play an important role. Besides its own uprights and grands, the factory builds or used to build instruments for brands like Astor, Bergmann, Knabe and Weber.

STEINWAY & SONS. **Bösendorfer** No list of 'famous' brands would be complete without the names Steinway and Bösendorfer. Both brands supply instruments in the highest price range only. Bösendorfer was founded in 1828 in Vienna, where the factory is still located (on a street called Bösendorferstrasse). Steinway has two factories: one in Hamburg, Germany (the original home of the family, then still called Steinweg) and one in America, where Steinway & Sons was founded in 1853. Boston (1991) is a cheaper Steinway brand built in Asia.

America

Baldwin, which sells pianos in the higher price range, is one of the most famous American names. The two cheaper brands produced by this company, **Wurlitzer** and **Chickering**, are rarely seen in Europe, as indeed are other American uprights and grand pianos including **Mason**

and Rich, Cable and Winter. Other famous brands, some no longer in production, are Steck, Meyer and Packard.

Asia

Asia has the world's largest musical instrument factories. A few well-known examples are the Guangzhou Piano Manufactory in China, with its own brand Pearl River, and the Korean firm Samick. Just like Kawai, Yamaha and Young Chang, Samick manufactures pianos in several countries, both in Asia and beyond. Virtually all Asian factories build instruments for several different makes. For instance, Chinese factories build pianos for brands like Nordiska, Carl Ebel and Richter which were originally European, as well as for the dozens of new Chinese brands. Two well-known Korean brands are Daewoo and Hyundai.

Germany

There are many other German brands besides the names listed above. A few well-known examples are Ibach (1794), the oldest surviving piano factory; Blüthner, featuring aliquot strings in the high treble of its grand pianos; Feurich, run by Julius Feurich (a member of the fifth generation of this family); Pfeiffer, which besides its own brands also carries the slightly lower-priced instruments of Hupfeld and Rönisch; Wilh. Steinberg, a medium-sized factory which, among its other models, produces Germany's cheapest upright; and Steingraeber, which builds the world's tallest upright piano at four and a half feet (138cm). The brands Brückner, Solton and Steinmann also come from Germany. Blüthner produces mid-priced instruments under the name Haessler.

Britain

One of the best-known British names is Kemble, a brand established in 1911 which has taken over the well-known firms Chappell and Collard and Collard. Whelpdale, founded in 1876 as an importer for Blüthner, supplies the smaller brands Knight, Bentley, Welmar, Marshal & Rose and Broadwood, famous as the makers of Beethoven's later pianos, among others. Woodchester is a very young company (1994), established in the former Bentley factory when this firm was taken over.

Poland

Th. Betting is one of the most famous Polish brands, although pianos are no longer produced under that name. The man who gave his name to the company, Theodor Betting, also founded the Polish firm **Schirmer & Sons**, a brand which is still in production. Other brands with Polish origins include **Fibiger**, **Calisia**, **Ravenstein** and **Steinbeck**. Poland also produces parts used by other manufacturers worldwide.

Czech Republic

As well as the larger companies named above, the Czech Republic has some smaller piano brands. Two examples are **Klima** and **Seidl**, the latter founded just a few years ago.

Other countries

There are piano manufacturers in many other countries too. One of the better-known examples is **Estonia**. This firm was founded in 1893 as the Tallinn Piano Factory in what is now the Estonian capital. Another is the much more expensive Italian make **Fazioli**. Fazioli builds the world's longest grand piano, the F 308. The uprights and grands of the German-sounding brands **Furstein** and **Schulze-Pollman** also come from Italy. **Bechner** and **Lippman** are two brands owned by a Dutch company; the instruments are made in the Ukraine.

GLOSSARY AND INDEX

This glossary briefly explains all the jargon touched upon so far. It also contains some words that haven't been mentioned yet, but which you may come across in magazines and brochures. The numbers refer to the page(s) that contain further information on the subject.

Acoustic piano The qualification 'acoustic' only became necessary after electric and (later) digital pianos had been invented – just as was the case with guitars. In other words, an acoustic piano is an 'ordinary', or as some say, a 'real' piano. Sometimes jokingly referred to as a steam piano.

Action (*7–9, 12, 29, 43–49, 66–67, 105–106*) All the wooden, felt, metal, leather and other parts which together ensure that when you play a piano's keys you set the hammers, strings and dampers in motion.

Agraffes (*57*) Brass string-guides.

Automatic piano (*83*) A modern player piano.

Baby grand (*31*) A small grand piano.

Backposts (*6–7, 40*) Wooden posts which give extra robustness to an upright piano. The equivalent posts in a grand piano are called braces.

Bass (*10, 52, 53, 77*) The lowest notes, produced by single-wound and double-wound strings.

Belly See: *Crown.*

Bench (*86–87*) See: *Stool.*

Bird-cage action See: *Overdamper.*

Boudoir grand Small to medium-sized grand piano.

Braces See: *Backposts*.

Bridge *(10, 55, 57)* The bridges (a short one for the bass strings and a long one for the rest) transmit the vibrations of the strings to the soundboard.

Capo d'astro (Capo Tasto) See: *Pressure bar*.

Castor cups *(18, 88–89)* Placed under a piano's castors to protect the floor, and sometimes to reduce sound transmission.

Castors *(36)* Piano wheels are often called castors.

Celeste pedal See: *Moderator, Practice pedal*.

Cheek blocks See: *Key blocks*.

Concert grand *(31)* A 'real' concert grand is about 9 feet long, sometimes more.

Console *(30)* Small type of upright. See: *Spinet*.

Covered strings See: *Wound strings*.

Cross-strung *(12, 70, 109)* Early pianos were *straight-strung*; by allowing the

strings to run diagonally so that the bass strings cross the other strings, longer strings can fit inside a smaller cabinet. Also called *overstrung*.

Crown *(60, 61, 95)* The arch of the soundboard. Also called the *belly*.

Dampers *(7, 8, 49–51)* Felt dampers mute the strings when you let go the keys after playing them.

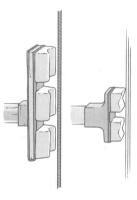

Large dampers for the bass strings, smaller ones for the higher-sounding strings

Descant See: *Treble*.

Digital piano *(18, 83–85)* A piano without strings; the sounds are samples (digital recordings).

Discant See: *Treble*.

Double-strike *(44, 67)* When a hammer 'bounces' against a string and strikes it twice (or more) when you don't want it to.

Down weight The force needed to play a soft note, expressed in grams. See also: *Up weight, Touch weight*.

Duplex scale *(59)* A system which allows the section of higher strings which is not struck to resonate and contribute to the tone.

End blocks See: *Key blocks*.

Escapement See: *Set-off*.

Even temperament *(103–105)* A particular tuning method.

Fall, fallboard The lid that covers the keyboard and protects it.

Flats The black keys.

Forte pedal See: *Right-hand pedal*.

Frame *(9, 115)* The cast-iron frame which, together with the backposts or braces, forms the backbone of an upright or grand piano. Also called the *plate*.

French polish *(32, 90–91)* Old-fashioned, expensive finish for pianos. The material used is shellac.

Front lid *(11, 39)* The front part of a grand piano lid.

Hammer heads, hammers *(5, 49–51, 67–68, 95, 105)* Piano strings are struck with felt hammers.

Hitch-pins *(54, 55, 58)* The strings run from the tuning-pins to the hitch-pins.

Hybrid piano *(82)* An acoustic piano with a built-in digital piano module.

Hygrometer *(95–98)* A device to measure humidity.

Jack *(7–9, 45, 63)* The jacks strike the hammers to send them towards the strings.

Key blocks *(94)* The small plateaus to the left and right of the keyboard. Also called *end blocks* or *cheek blocks*.

Key dip *(43)* Every key must have the same key dip: you must be able to press each one down the same distance.

Keyboard *(4, 5–6, 37, 42–43, 84, 117)* Usually has eighty-eight keys, although some older keyboards have eighty-five. See also: *Keys*.

Keys *(42–43, 91)* The keyboard usually has fifty-two ivory or synthetic-covered white keys and thirty-six synthetic or wood black keys.

Laminated See: *Solid wood.*

Lamp *(87–88)* A good piano lamp gives a good distribution of light.

Left-hand pedal *(5, 12, 63, 65)* The left-hand pedal of an upright moves the hammers closer to the strings, which makes everything sound softer. For this reason it's also called the soft pedal. On grand pianos, the left-hand pedal works differently. See: *Una corda pedal.*

Let-off See: *Set-off.*

Lid *(5, 6, 37–40, 93)* An upright piano has a hinged lid which either opens completely or is made in two parts, in which case the front part opens. The lid of a grand piano always consists of two parts, the front lid and the main lid. The lid of a grand piano is sometimes called the *top.*

Lid prop *(40)* The lid prop keeps the lid of a grand piano open. Also called *top stick.*

Lower panel *(5, 92)* The panel which encloses the part of the piano below the keyboard.

Lyre *(11, 12, 65)* The pedals of a grand piano pivot in the lyre.

Mechanism See: *Action.*

Metronome *(19–20, 80)* Sets a tempo with ticks or bleeps.

Middle pedal See: *Moderator, Practice pedal* and *Sostenuto pedal.*

MIDI *(81–82, 85)* A system which allows digital musical instruments and equipment to communicate with each other. Pianos can be equipped with MIDI too.

Moderator *(6, 17, 64–65)* A moderator is a strip of felt which can be lowered between the hammers and the strings to mute the strings, usually with a *practice pedal*, but sometimes operated by hand. Also called a *celeste pedal.*

Music panel See: *Upper panel.*

Music shelf *(39–40)* The panel of a grand piano which holds the music stand.

Music stand *(5, 6, 38, 39)* Pianos always have a built-in music stand.

Muting system *(18, 65, 79, 80, 82)* If your piano has a muting system, you can practice on it without anyone hearing you.

Naturals The white keys.

Octave *(4–5, 12–13)* A piano keyboard has a good seven octaves.

Open pore *(32, 90)* Instrument on which the grain (pores) of the wood can still be felt.

Overdamper *(69)* An old model of upright piano in which the dampers are above the hammers. Also called *bird-cage action*.

Overstrung See: *Cross-strung*.

Pedals *(5–6, 12, 62–66)* Pianos have two or three pedals. The right-hand pedal removes all the dampers from the strings, the left-hand pedal makes everything sound softer. The middle pedal is usually a practice pedal on uprights and a sostenuto pedal on grands. See: *Left-hand pedal, Right-hand pedal, Moderator, Practice pedal* and *Sostenuto pedal*.

Piano pedal See: *Left-hand pedal*.

Pianola See: *Player piano*.

Pinblock *(10, 56, 69)* The tuning-pins are set into a hardwood pinblock. Also called *wrest plank*.

Plate See: *Frame*.

Player piano *(110)* A piano that plays itself. The modern version works digitally. The name *Pianola* is also in use, but this is in fact a registered trademark for player pianos made by Aeolian.

Polyester lacquer *(31–32, 90–91, 94, 117)* Most pianos are finished with polyester lacquer.

Practice pedal See: *Moderator*.

Pressure bar *(58)* Strings are held in place either by a pressure bar (or *capo d'astro, capo bar*) or by *agraffes*. See also: *Agraffes*.

Ribs *(6–7, 61, 69)* Wooden bars which reinforce the soundboard and give it its arch, and help it transmit sound more effectively.

Right-hand pedal *(5, 62–63)* Removes the dampers from the strings so that all the notes you play continue to sound. Other names: *sustain pedal, sustaining* *pedal, damper pedal, loud pedal.*

Rim *(42)* The 'cabinet' of a grand piano.

Satin-finish *(31, 90–91)* Satin-finish instruments have a transparent silk-gloss or eggshell lacquer.

Scale *(53)* Everything connected with the choice of strings is collectively called the scale: the thickness and the length, the number of strings, the winding...

Shellac See: *French polish.*

School piano *(36)* A piano with protective brackets, large wheels and extra locks.

Secondhand buying tips *(23–24, 67–70)*

Serial number *(70)* You can work out the age of a piano from its serial number.

Set-off *(44, 45)* Many different aspects of the action need to be regulated carefully. The set-off is one of them. Also called *let-off* and *escapement.*

Sharps *(42)* See: *Flats.*

Solid wood *(62, 115)* Most soundboards are made of planks of solid spruce. Other parts (pinblocks, for instance) are virtually always laminated *(56, 62).*

Sostenuto pedal *(12, 65, 66)* Middle pedal of a grand piano which sustains only those notes being played when it is pressed. Also called *Steinway pedal.*

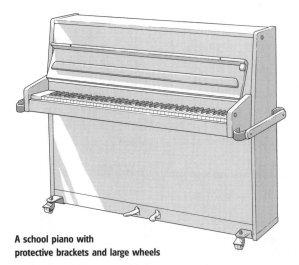

A school piano with protective brackets and large wheels

Sound module *(18, 79–81)* A box containing digital recordings (samples) of a piano or other instruments.

Soundboard *(6–7, 29, 30, 60, 69, 70, 95, 115)* The soul of a piano. The soundboard amplifies the sound of the strings.

Speaking length *(53, 59)* The part of the string which vibrates, producing a note, when struck with a hammer. See also *Duplex scale.*

Spinet *(30)* 1. Spinet piano. The very smallest upright piano (up to some 40" or 100cm high). *(107)* 2. An early keyboard instrument with mechanically plucked strings.

Spun strings See: *Wound strings.*

Steinway pedal See: *Sostenuto pedal.*

Stool *(86–87)* Piano stools come in various designs, many of which can have their height adjusted.

Straight-strung See: *Cross-strung.*

Stringing studs See: *Agraffes.*

Strings *(9, 29, 52–55, 68, 115–116)* A piano has around two hundred and twenty steel strings. Only the lowest bass notes have one string each. The upper bass notes have two strings each: the two-string unisons *(9, 51, 52, 53)*. From the first low treble notes upwards there are three strings per note: the three-string unisons *(9, 51, 52, 53)*.

Studio piano *(30)* Medium- to large-size upright piano.

Studs See: *Agraffes.*

Sustain pedal, sustaining pedal See: *Right-hand pedal.*

Swivel-top stool *(86, 87)* A height-adjustable, round piano stool.

Tenor See: *Treble.*

Top See: *Lid.*

Top stick See: *Lid prop.*

Touch weight *(46)* The force needed to keep a key in motion, a function of the *down weight* and *up weight.*

Treble *(10, 52, 53, 77)* The highest five octaves (approximately) of a piano, sometimes divided into low treble or tenor (c–c2; see page 13) and high treble (discant, descant), the latter referring to the highest three octaves.

Tuning *(27, 68–69, 100–103)* A piano needs to be tuned regularly: a job for an expert!

Tuning-pins *(10, 55–58, 69)* Steel pins used to tune the strings. Also called *wrest pins*.

Una corda pedal *(12, 65–66)* The left-hand pedal of a grand piano; gives a softer, but also a slightly different tone.

Underdamper All modern upright pianos are under-dampers: the dampers are under the hammers. See also: *Overdamper*.

Unison See: *Strings*.

Up weight *(45, 46)* The force with which a key comes back up. See also: *Touchweight*.

Upper panel *(5, 6, 33, 39)* The panel right in front of you when you are playing an upright. Also called the *music panel*.

Voicing *(51, 105, 118)* Treating the hammer heads to make the instrument sound as good as possible. *Rough voicing* is one of the stages a piano goes through at the factory.

Wheels See: *Castors*.

Wound strings *(10, 52)* The bass strings are wound with copper wire; this allows them to sound low enough without becoming too long. Also called *wrapped strings*, *covered strings* and *spun strings*.

Wrapped strings See: *Wound strings*.

Wrest pins See: *Tuning-pins*.

Wrest plank See: *Pinblock*.

WANT TO KNOW MORE?

There are many places to read more about pianos. There are various magazines, stacks of books on every aspect of the instrument, and of course a lot of information on the Internet too.

MAGAZINES

A number of different magazines aimed at pianists are available, usually containing interviews, articles about pianists and composers, CD reviews, sheet music and pieces about technique and maintenance.

- *Piano & Keyboard*, Sparrowhawk Press, Inc., 223 San Anselmo Avenue, Ste. 8, San Anselmo, CA 94960, phone (415) 458-8672, (415) 458-2955
- *Piano Today*, 333 Adams Street, Bedford Hills, NY 10507, phone (914) 244-8500, fax (914) 244-8560
- *Piano*, Rhinegold Publishing Ltd., 241 Shaftesbury Avenue, London W2CH 8EH, phone 020 7333 1724, fax 020 7333 1769.

BOOKS

There are dozens of books on pianos, from fat volumes on the history and workings of the instrument to lavishly illustrated coffee-table books, and books with extensive descriptions of the way pianos are built. A very limited selection is given below.

- *The Piano Book – Buying & Owning a New or Used Piano*, Larry Fine (Brookside Press, Boston, 1994). Very comprehensive book which discusses at greater length many of the matters touched on in *The Rough Guide to Piano*. A special feature is that the latest updates to the text can be found on the Internet (www.tiac.net/users/pianobk).